"This guide combines the
spectful approach to the complexities of stepfamily life.
Drawing on her own experiences, Natalie walks us through
behind-the-scenes events and moves us to a realistic notion
while inspiring us to live more creatively within a Christian
stepfamily."

Dr. Margorie Engel, president and CEO,
Stepfamily Association of America

"I can't imagine that a little girl who dreams of being a wife
and a mother dreams of that picture in the context of a
blended family. What she hopes for is a commitment that
lasts a lifetime. Unfortunately, given our human nature and
the reality that some very good lessons are learned the hard
way, many of us find ourselves starting over in the context of
a blended family. Just as any two people are different, every
relationship and every family comes with its own unique
dynamic. Sometimes hearing about another person's journey
can re-energize us in the midst of our own. There is no road
map for navigating a blended family, but Natalie Gillespie's
insights are helpful, interesting, and encouraging. Here's to
the journey . . ."

Amy Grant, recording artist

"After writing novels for teens for so many years I've often
been asked about resources for blended families. I'm thrilled
that Natalie has provided such a book! She comes to this
project with first hand experience and a great heart toward
the challenges of stepfamily survival."

Robin Jones Gunn, bestselling author of The Christy
Miller series and the Sisterchicks™ novels

"Natalie Nichols Gillespie scores a home run in *Stepfamily Sucess*. If God has led you into the blended family adventure, you're sure to glean a wealth of information and inspiration from these pages."

Angela Hunt, author of *The Debt*

"Finally, a book to help blended families navigate their way through the inevitable problems they'll be faced with. What I love about *Stepfamily Success* is that it has real solutions, not just warnings. I wish I'd had it so much earlier!"

Terri Blackstock, author of *Cape Refuge*, *Southern Storm*, and *River's Edge*

"Natalie has given us an honest and practical look at how to *thrive* in everyday life, not just survive. I love the solution suggestions and discussion questions—this is real life in action! And real life can be wonderful when families strategically work together, anticipate life's hurdles and above all make every effort to preserve the wholeness and stability of the children."

Tammy Gallegos Bennett, founder, Christian CoParenting After Divorce

Stepfamily
SUCCESS

Practical Solutions
for Common Challenges

Natalie Nichols Gillespie

© 2004 by Natalie Nichols Gillespie

Published by Revell
a division of Baker Publishing Group
P.O. Box 6287, Grand Rapids, MI 49516-6287
www.revellbooks.com

Spire edition published 2007
ISBN 10: 0-8007-8755-2
ISBN 978-0-8007-8755-4

Previously published in 2004 as *The Stepfamily Survival Guide*

Printed in the United States of America

This book is lovingly dedicated to Adam, the man God placed in my life to be my soul mate, the world's best dad, and a gourmet cook so that our family doesn't starve.

To Lorra, Leigha, and Lydia, three girls who entered my life and changed it forever in the best possible way when I married their dad. Thank you for all you have taught me and for the privilege of loving you.

To Jessica and Joshua, my firstborn children. It was love at first sight, and you still have my heart.

To Justin, "Cowboy Roy," the funny little man who is the glue in our stepfamily, the one person we all have in common. You're the best, Bud.

And to Amberlie Joy Fu Shuang, the precious baby girl from China who stole all our hearts.

Contents

Foreword

Complaints are hard to listen to. For years I listened to the complaints of disillusioned single parents and stepfamily couples who were frustrated that there weren't more faith-based books for stepfamilies. Truly, I began to recognize there was a significant gap in the Christian family literature—and something needed to change.

With my 2002 release of *The Smart Stepfamily: Seven Steps to a Healthy Family*, I was honored to contribute to the growing list of books for stepfamilies. I am again honored to be associated (even if only in this small way) with another significant contribution—the release of this book.

Developing a stepfamily is a journey that is wrought with mountains to climb and unmapped territory to forge. Surviving the journey takes patience, perseverance, and at times, unswerving determination. It also helps to have a survival guide—like this one. In this book, Natalie Nichols Gillespie weaves together personal experience, humor, and practical tools for surviving the stepfamily journey. And she does so with God at the center. You've picked up a gem. By all means, start reading...

Ron L. Deal
Director, Successful Stepfamilies

Acknowledgments

This book is a real labor of love, and I'd like to thank those who encouraged me along the way:

To Adam—thanks for reading and re-reading and for being my loving partner in everything, and to all our kids for bearing with me on writing days.

To Margaret Feinberg, a fellow author and true friend; to Brian Peterson—thank you for believing I had this book in me and for presenting it to the Baker team; to Paul Brinker-hoff, Lonnie Hull DuPont, and Laura Weller for such careful and thorough edits and suggestions. To Ron Deal, for such dedication to stepfamilies, and to Dr. Margorie Engel, president of the Stepfamily Association of America, for helping me incorporate some of the best stepfamily practices into my writing.

To my dad, Gordon Nichols, who always told me I could do anything; and to my sisters and brother, Noelle Hall, Nicole Loden, and GordonLee Nichols for cheering me on. To my mom in heaven, Jeri, I miss you!

To my ex-husband, Mark Steven Woolbright, 1967–2006. He left behind a legacy of love for his children and was a great co-parent with me. To Kathe Woolbright, my kids' stepmom, thanks for making co-parenting easy, and for still loving our kids even now that Mark is gone. To Mark's parents, Billy and Frances Chain (my loving "out-laws") for accepting all of my family as part of your family.

And to my Savior, who always picks me up, brushes me off, and sets me on my feet again.

Introduction

While there are few current statistics to show exactly how many Americans have experienced divorce or are part of a stepfamily, some studies show that slightly more than half of all first marriages in America end in divorce. About 75 percent of divorced persons remarry, and about 60 percent of all remarriages end in divorce.[1]

Family experts believe that half of all Americans are now or will be a stepparent, a stepchild, a stepsibling, or some other member of a stepfamily. More than half of all Americans today have been, are now, or will eventually be in one or more step situations, and more than thirteen hundred stepfamilies are being formed in the United States *every day*.[2]

Christians are not immune to divorce and remarriage, as evidenced by statistics that equal or surpass those of non-Christians. Whether we like it or not, millions of American Christians are dealing with the painful issues that accompany failed marriages, remarriages, and stepfamilies. They are the families sitting next to you in the pew each Sunday. They are the kids playing with your kids in the nursery each week. They are the moms you visit with every Tuesday in your Bible study. They may be your family. They are my family too.

In the Christian community—even in the most well-meaning of churches—there is often a lack of stepfamily mentoring and ministry. Christians creating second families are often too afraid of rejection to share the struggles they face and the pain they experience. They put on a happy face on Sunday mornings, then cry all the way home from church.

I began researching and writing this book when I could not find a Christian resource that could help me with the challenges our family faced as we began "step"ping together. I hope it will give other stepfamilies reassurance and encouragement. Although there are huge relationship mountains to climb, the view is breathtaking from the top—and you will make it to the other side if you persevere!

I am not a trained professional in the field of family counseling, but if doing something day in and day out for more than five years truly makes you an "expert" at it, then I am an expert at being part of a stepfamily. Most days I sure don't feel like one. Chances are, you don't either.

My three stepdaughters, their mom and stepdad, and my husband and I went through agonizing custody litigation. It took three years and four judges, three guardian ad litems, three psychologists, one psychiatrist, and several agencies before custody was decided. It was excruciatingly painful for everyone involved and exacted a high price emotionally, spiritually, and relationally, not to mention tens of thousands of dollars financially. It was the most difficult thing I have ever been through, even more painful than the breakup of my first marriage.

My husband and I have young children who adore us and teenagers who often think they hate us. We have one adult child who has little contact with us and a first-grader who says he is never leaving us. As parents and stepparents, we have laughed uproariously and sobbed uncontrollably over our family. At times we have yelled angrily; at other times we have whispered adoringly over each of these beautiful, unique children God has entrusted us to guide toward him.

I say all of this up front to let you know that we are not the perfect stepfamily. Far from it. But we are a stepfamily covered by God's grace, immersed in his mercy. Through our family's ups and downs, we have actively witnessed his hand at work in our lives.

Successful stepfamilies can become reality, for God is a Redeemer. He is *our* Redeemer. And that means he is perfectly capable of redeeming families, not only nuclear families in trouble but also stepfamilies like mine and yours, to have the special grace, patience, and favor to become—through our love and strength under adversity—a powerful witness for him.

Within these pages you will find practical advice for stepfamilies that is centered around a Christian perspective and biblical worldview. I know that each stepfamily is unique, and not every piece of advice will be appropriate or possible for every stepfamily. For example, my husband and I both brought children to our marriage, which is a completely different circumstance than stepfamilies where it is the first marriage for one of the partners, while the other has been married before and has children.

Whatever your stepfamily story, I believe this book can provide positive tools to guide your stepfamily towards a firm footing.

As you read, you will notice that I only use the terms *parent* and *stepparent*. In keeping with current research and the best practices recommended by the Stepfamily Association of America, only those two terms are necessary. Words like *biological*, *natural*, and *original* parent are intentionally avoided so that families are not divided unnecessarily. The term *blended* is also not used in this book, as stepfamilies do not blend into something entirely new, leaving all the old behind. Stepfamily research suggests that *blended* is a term to avoid, and while I realize that stepfamilies sometimes prefer to call themselves "blended," I have made the effort not to use that terminology within my book.

My prayer is that this book will be a starting point for you as a stepfamily, a great encouragement for what you are already doing right, and at the very least, a reminder that you are not alone.

Part One
THE MARRIAGE

1

Blessed Be the Ties That Bind, Even When They Unravel

"For I know the plans I have for you," declares the Lord, "plans to prosper you and not to harm you, plans to give you hope and a future."

—Jeremiah 29:11

Congratulations! If you have picked up this book, you are probably part of a stepfamily, you grew up in a stepfamily, or you are planning to start a stepfamily. You are blessed indeed! No, I am not kidding.

Being part of this unique kind of family situation is a tremendous gift, privilege, and blessing. Don't let anybody tell you otherwise. Our stepfamily of six children and two adults is the best thing that ever happened to me. It is challenging, some days seemingly overwhelming, many times gut-wrenching, but it has taught me much about the fullness of life. It has opened my eyes to more lessons about grace, mercy, and true love than I ever dreamed possible.

Stepfamilies have long had a bad reputation. They are not traditional, *Leave It to Beaver*–type, nuclear families consisting of a man and a woman who marry and bring forth children and live happily ever after. Stepfamilies, instead, are birthed most often out of the tremendous heartache and contention that come with death or divorce.

While it is true that stepfamilies are created from loss and face tremendous challenges, I have learned through experience that this in no way means they are destined to remain "less than" a traditional family. Even through divorce, betrayal, ongoing litigation, false accusations, children who don't like you or each other, former spouses, and the ordinary pressures of daily life, stepfamilies can make it and be a blessing to one another. Yes, the pressure can be enormous, but that same pressure can mold your stepfamily into a new creation, one that glorifies Christ and loves one another.

A harmonious stepfamily is not the impossible dream. Getting there takes a lot of slow baby steps. Some days you will slide backward and have to work even harder to regain lost ground. But progress *can* be made. I know—I live it every hour of every day.

In the Beginning

I was raised in a charismatic Christian family by parents who got "turned on" to Jesus during the 1970s, formed a weekly prayer group that met for eleven years, and prayed for me endlessly. I am the oldest of four children, and my parents never divorced. Their parents never divorced. None of our friends or family members ever divorced. It wasn't until the mid-1980s, when I was in ninth grade, that I even met anyone whose parents were getting divorced!

I was "Miss Academic" all through my childhood, sailing straight from elementary school through a bachelor's degree with A's in nearly every subject. But somewhere along the road—at about age sixteen or so—I decided I wanted to try things my way.

I wanted to drive the car of my own life and, quite frankly, expected God to ride quietly in the backseat. By the time I was in college, I forgot he was even around. I guess I figured he had gotten out somewhere along the way and was maybe riding a couple of cars behind me. I knew he was still there somewhere; I trusted him for my salvation and argued with him daily about where my car keys were hiding, but I didn't care to ask his opinion on the bigger issues, like how to live for him instead of myself, whether I was going too far sexually, and if any of the men I dated was the "right" one for me.

After college I married a man I now firmly believe the Lord had *not* chosen for me (or me for him) and watched our life and our marriage fall apart all around us in just three short years. I finally handed the wreck I had made of my once-shiny-sports-car life back to the Lord and pleaded with him to put it—like Humpty Dumpty—back together again. He graciously obliged, but, boy, did it hurt. The anger of betrayal, the anguish of a broken heart, and the utter shame of getting As in English and calculus only to get a big, fat F-minus in life experiences created extreme emotional pain, which I hope was the closest thing to hell I will ever experience.

It took a long time to put the pieces back together again, but during that time of aloneness and loneliness, I finally stopped whining to the Lord about my ex-husband always seeming to have someone in his life and about my being all alone with two tiny kids. I began to trust my Savior with my life, not just my eternity. The turning point came when I heard the Lord clearly ask me one night while I was driving home from my job of reviewing theater productions and rock 'n' roll concerts for a daily newspaper: "Where are you spending your time that you could meet the man I have for you? You are my child, and I don't want to see you in this pain again."

Whoa! That was an eye-opener. I worked in a church nursery on Sundays to earn extra money and hadn't attended an actual service in years. I had few Christian friends and no fellowship, and I could blow dust off of my long-unopened Bible. I spent my days at the newspaper and my evenings with my kids or at work as a critic watching rock 'n' roll concerts and theater productions (where the audience attended as couples and the players were often of questionable sexual orientation). Even *I* could see that these were probably not the places where my dedicated-to-the-Lord Prince Charming was going to ride up on his white horse and carry me off, with my kids tucked gingerly into saddlebags on the sides, into the sunset.

After much prayer, pleading, and seeking, I left my job at the newspaper, took my divorce papers, my humiliation and shame, my sense of failure, my broken heart, my three-year-old daughter, my four-month-old son, and a U-Haul filled with my portion of the material possessions of my broken life, and drove thirteen hundred miles away from Oklahoma to my home state of Florida to finish licking my wounds. And that's where the Lord really got hold of my heart again. When I found myself at the very bottom emotionally, there was nowhere to look but up. I needed him, and I was ready to admit it and hand over control, even if he was going to say, "I told you so."

Can I let you in on a secret? He didn't.

Instead, with infinite tenderness and mercy, the Lord lovingly embraced me, restored my trust in humanity—and later in myself—and healed my hurting heart.

Starting Over: Beginning to Build

That's where Adam came in. He didn't ride up on a white horse. Instead, we sat next to each other in church one Sunday. Only a couple of weeks later, during the closing benediction when we all joined hands across the aisle, he laced his fingers through mine rather than clasping my palm, and I *knew*. The rest was history.

Adam's side of the story in a nutshell is that after ten years in a first marriage and a three-year divorce process, he too spent time grieving and healing, seeking spiritually to find a place of peace. When he felt "ready" emotionally for a new relationship, he asked the Lord for a small favor. "I know your Word says you want to give us the desires of our hearts," Adam prayed, "so while we are talking, could I ask for a tall, thin blonde, never married, no kids?"

He didn't get an audible response right away, but the next Sunday there I was in the pew—all five feet, three inches of nicely rounded, previously married, dark-brown-haired me, my two small children checked into the preschool nurseries down the hall. I wasn't what Adam ordered, but I was the perfect fit. After all, who do you think created us with a sense of humor?

Almost one year later, with our families' and the Lord's approval, we joined hands again in front of an audience of our combined five children, ranging in age at that time from eighteen months to thirteen years, and 125 of our closest family and friends. Our wedding invitations asked guests to witness the marriage of "Natalie, Jessica, and Joshua" to "Adam, Lorra, Leigha, and Lydia." Our pastor included the children in a closing prayer during our wedding ceremony, right after we recited our vows. He asked God's blessing in binding us together as a new family. Adam and I vowed to love each other forever with God's help.

Fast-forward eight years, one custody battle, one mutual child, Justin, and one twelve-passenger van later, and we are living mostly happily in the forever after. Our children now range in age from six to twenty-one, and we spend our days driving back and forth to schools, Girl Scouts, piano lessons, co-ops, martial arts, and parent-teacher conferences.

As parents and stepparents, Adam and I never quite get used to sending two of our girls to their other stepfamily every other weekend, on half of the holidays, and for five weeks every summer. We agonize over sending a daughter and son on a thirteen-hundred-mile trek to Tulsa, Oklahoma, each summer to spend their vacation with their other stepfamily, while the kids rejoice at seeing family they get to spend time with only once or twice a year. We feel guilty at any sense of excitement when the house is quieter than usual because some of them are gone. And we struggle daily to find adequate family time, because our children's time is divided among three households and various schools and activities.

Our children have half-siblings and stepsiblings in each of their homes, so they must switch their birth order roles regularly. Sometimes they are the oldest children, sometimes the middle. The former baby of the family is now a middle child in both households. The youngest of four daughters in our home is the only girl in the middle of four boys at her dad's house. Phew! Quite frankly, it's a lot to keep straight.

Some days our kids think they are lucky to have two moms and dads who love them, two sets of Christmases and birthdays to celebrate. Some days they are unbearably sad, wishing there were two of them to be in both homes at once. Oftentimes they are angry that life was interrupted, that their family structure has changed. Many times they rebel, having quickly learned how to "work" the system, giving the

---

A stepfamily is somewhat like oil and water. You can mix us up, but eventually we tend to settle back into our original positions. What I have learned, sometimes the hard way, is that *this settling is normal and okay*.

---

absent parent only their side of the story, knowing that the communication barriers between their divorced parents will gain them sympathy even when they are wrong.

We are a stepfamily, and we are not picture-perfect by any stretch of the imagination. I would like to call us a "blended family," but that can be misleading. While we have moments, even entire days, when we come together beautifully, a stepfamily is somewhat like oil and water. You can mix us up, but eventually we tend to settle back into our original positions. What I have learned, sometimes the hard way, is that *this settling is normal and okay*. I have learned that light that tries to shine through blends is murky, but light that God moves through oil and water can create shimmering patterns of beautiful, unique color and character.

Handing It Over: He Understands

God can do that with your stepfamily too. He *will* do that, for the Lord knows firsthand what it is like to be different than the nuclear family. Jesus was adopted by Joseph, and had half-brothers and half-sisters. Think about the challenges he, his parents, and his siblings faced:

- Jesus had an adopted father in Joseph.
- Jesus had half-siblings and must have known what it felt like not to fit in completely.
- Joseph often must have felt inadequate, wondering if he could ever live up to his Son's Father. Think of what it would have been like to have absolute perfection, the Creator of the universe, as the other guy.
- Jesus' half-sisters and half-brothers sometimes must have found it difficult to like this child who came first, who was obviously different, who they must have instinctively known would always outshine them.
- Mary must have wondered how to strike a balance in her home, how to keep peace, and how to rear her children with enough love to cover their differences.

By sending his only Son to live in a situation similar to our stepfamilies, I believe God showed his love for our stepfamilies. He might hate divorce, but he loves mending broken lives that are laid at his feet. He knows your pain; he understands your struggles.

I do too. I understand the pain you feel when your children hurt because of the consequences of your actions. I also understand the sheer joy found in forgiveness, the weight of guilt that flies away when emotional pain is healed.

I know what it is like to wonder if you are treating your own children differently than your stepchildren—to be afraid of being too easy on your kids and actually becoming too harsh.

Even now, after nearly a decade of being their stepmom, I still wonder if my stepdaughters will ever experience the emotional freedom to throw their arms around me and tell

---

By sending his only Son to live in a situation similar to our stepfamilies, I believe God showed his love for our stepfamilies. He might hate divorce, but he loves mending broken lives that are laid at his feet.

---

me they love me without feeling as if they are betraying their mom. I wonder if I will ever get over my hurt feelings when I work hard for them and they don't seem to care.

I wonder if we will eventually all live in peace. I pray that we will. Prayer is the greatest tool for most situations in life but especially for stepfamilies. So many situations for parents of stepfamilies are out of our control. Whether the problem is caused by a judge limiting contact with our children or by a former spouse inflicting emotional damage on those precious children we share, prayer can cover it. God does not always answer immediately or the way we want him to, but we can firmly grab hold of the peace that passes all understanding (see Phil. 4:7) when we release the situation into his hands.

God is always in control, even when the odds seem overwhelmingly stacked against us. He is our "ever-present help in trouble" (Ps. 46:1), which means that he is right there with us on the witness stand, he is with us in the midst of heated arguments with our teenagers, and he is with us in the middle of the night when we sob out our pain. He loved us enough to put us together as a stepfamily, knowing that if we can stand firm and hold on, we will have a testimony that cannot be shaken. And we can spread the Good News to other stepfamilies on the verge of falling apart.

Maybe the best advice I can give no matter what your situation is to pray that the dysfunction stops here, that the enemy may have no power over your household, and that the legacy left to your children may promote an intact family line and may restore the damage done to young lives.

Finally, while you pray without ceasing, stop beating yourself up over the past, teach your children from your mistakes without dwelling on them endlessly, and get busy living with joy "the good life which [God] prearranged and made ready for us to live" (Eph. 2:10 AMP).

2

Look Both Ways Before Crossing the Threshold

> Show me the path where I should go, O Lord;
>   point out the road for me to walk. . . .
> And when we obey him, every path he guides us
>   on is fragrant with his lovingkindness and his
>   truth.
>
> —Psalm 25:4, 10 TLB

Our True Love Story

After we had been dating for about eight months, Adam and I started talking about marriage but had not yet formalized anything. One afternoon in the spring of 1996, Adam had a court hearing regarding visitation with his three daughters. I accompanied him to court, a sign of true love if ever there was one. After a grueling afternoon in front of the judge, we were walking through the corridors when I jokingly suggested that since we were already at the courthouse, we should pop into the clerk's office and get our marriage license.

Adam replied, "Okay, let's do it!"

I immediately felt that I had overstepped my bounds; I never expected that he would take my suggestion seriously. He hadn't even proposed. He began tugging on my hand, though, pulling me toward the clerk's office. Still thinking it was all a joke, I resisted. Adam went into the office alone.

After a few minutes, Adam returned and grabbed my hand again. This time he did pull me into the office, shouting, "I found one! I found one!" as we entered the door. What I did not know was that when Adam had gone in the first time, he had asked for a marriage license and the clerk at the counter had asked him where his bride was.

"Oh! I have to have one of those picked out already?" Adam asked, acting puzzled.

"Yes, the licenses are only good for sixty days, you know, and your bride has to sign the license when you apply," the clerk replied.

"Keep that license ready then, and I'll be right back," Adam told the now plainly confused woman behind the counter.

That's when he came back into the hall and got me. When he reentered the door, shouting "I found one!" and waving our clasped hands in the air in triumph, the women behind their desks stopped working and actually clapped and cheered!

When I saw that this God-honoring man whom I already knew I loved deeply was a man who could also make a roomful of tired women laugh at the end of a long workday, I knew he couldn't be all bad. I signed that license, and we had sixty days to pull off a wedding.

We invited our family and some friends to a service on June 1, 1996, in the little chapel of the First Baptist Church of Indian Rocks in Largo, Florida, where the Lord first introduced us by way of that hand-holding benediction. We mailed the invitations that requested the honor of our guests' presence at the marriage of Adam, Lorra, Leigha, and Lydia to Natalie, Jessica, and Joshua. How beautiful those names looked to me all linked together on that paper. How neatly they fit, just like we would fit in our new life.

Ha! Little did I know.

On our wedding day as I was inside the bridal dressing room preparing to walk down the aisle, someone handed me a greeting card. I could tell from the handwriting on the envelope that it was from my sweet soon-to-be husband. I opened it, expecting a Hallmark gushing with silly sentiment over the new life we had ahead of us. Instead, Adam, ever the joker, had picked out a sympathy card offering me his condolences—and a one-dollar bill. (Adam said he was always disappointed growing up whenever a card did not have any money in it.) I laughed, a little puzzled, shrugged it off, and soon stepped lightly down the aisle to meet my groom and our children and to ride off into the sunset to live happily ever after.

If I had known then how many tears would be shed along this road toward the ever-elusive goal of "blended family," I would have realized how appropriate that sympathy card was.

Look Before You Leap

By the grace of God, Adam and I did one thing right before we married: we took time to heal in between our previous marriages and other dating relationships and the time we met and began dating. We didn't even know it was something we should do, but we were both prompted by the Lord to do it. Yes, we made mistakes. In the initial rush to rebuild self-esteem, we dated too soon after our divorces, and we dated the wrong people.

Then, half a country away from each other and before our introduction at church, we each got off the dating merry-go-round. We just knew it was time to be alone. Were we lonely? Yes, sometimes unbearably so, or so it seemed. Yet it wasn't until we could find peace in having only the Lord for comfort and to fill that void in our hearts that he deemed us ready to find each other.

After every divorce or the death of a spouse, it is crucial that newly single parents take time alone to heal. They need

---

Taking time alone, even though you will inevitably experience tremendous feelings of loneliness, can help ensure that you will see clearly when you begin taking steps to build a new life with a new partner.

---

time to grieve over their lost partner, time to be angry over the unfairness of life, time to learn to forgive themselves for their mistakes, time to comfort and reassure their children, time to get their relationship straightened out with the Lord, and time to allow him to bathe them in his love and reassurance before they run into the waiting arms of anyone who will help share their load.

> After every divorce or the death of a spouse, it is crucial that newly single parents take time alone to heal.

Children who have suffered the loss of an original family through death or divorce also need time to go through the grieving process before a new adult is introduced into their lives. Taking time alone, even though you will inevitably experience tremendous feelings of loneliness, can help ensure that you will see clearly when you begin taking steps to build a new life with a new partner.

On the flip side, once you are certain God has put you together with a partner for life, do not be afraid to forge ahead. As licensed marriage and family therapist Ron Deal shares in his book *The Smart Stepfamily*:

> Couples can create mutually satisfying, intimate, God-honoring marriages within stepfamilies. . . . Furthermore, I've observed that couples that endure the adversity of the journey, frequently have a bond that is powerful enough to withstand anything. There is strength and a sense of victory after surviving what for some is a difficult journey.[1]

Deal points out that stepfamily advantages can include the following:

- marital satisfaction
- healthy marriage models for children
- role models for children
- restored well-being in children
- adaptability and flexibility
- mistakes, lessons learned, and healing
- personal growth and spiritual commitment

Statistics show that many stepfamilies do not make it past the first two to three years. Keep that in mind when times get tough, and eliminate the word *divorce* from your vocabulary as you begin your new marriage.

Common Problems to Consider

After a divorce, single moms and dads are left with such battered self-esteem that they feel extremely grateful for anyone new who seems to care. This can lead to relationships becoming too serious, too fast. New relationships can be emotionally intoxicating and easily confused with real love if not tempered by time and the Holy Spirit. Single moms and dads also can be so overwhelmed with responsibilities that they jump into a relationship that isn't exactly what God has chosen for them because it is such a relief to have someone around who wants to help share their load.

Solution Suggestions

- If you have recently experienced a divorce or the death of a spouse, spend time alone—not away from family and friends, but without a romantic or potentially romantic relationship. Don't jump on the dating merry-go-round too soon.

- Set aside specific portions of each day to spend time alone with the Lord, searching his Word daily for comfort, allowing him to truly be your spouse (see Isa. 54:5) by welcoming his love for you. Be still in his presence. Run to him with your pain and anger, and let him deal with it.

- Don't withdraw from those who love you. Surround yourself with accountability partners, friends, and family who can let you cry on their shoulders, relieve some of your responsibilities, and give you a much needed break from time to time.

Often partners who enter a second marriage have not taken enough time to heal emotionally from wounds left by the first marriage. Without healing, they react negatively to the new spouse when thrust into any situation that "feels like" one from the past marriage. Frequently, there are also unresolved issues that caused the first marriage to destruct. Unless these issues are faced, they will likely surface again over time in a new relationship.

Solution Suggestions

- If anger seems uncontrollable, if you are taking your anger out on your kids or feel unable to care for them, or if you are dealing with such grief that you have ongoing symptoms of depression, find a grief counselor, a pastor, or a mental health professional who can give you tools for dealing with your overwhelming emotions. Only when you learn what triggered the dysfunction in the past will you be ready for a healthy future without running into the same brick walls.

- When you find yourself having the same arguments in a new relationship that you had in the old one, there is an unresolved issue that needs to be addressed. Are you still failing to trust? Do you want too much control? Are you replaying a hurt from your childhood in your adult relationships? Ask God to point out your strengths and weaknesses and to replace your faults with his peace.

- Listen to the advice of those who love you. Friends and family members who love you are on your side and want what is best for you. If more than one close person in your life sense that you are not ready for a new relationship or tell you that they see difficulties with any relationship you have started, see these warnings as red flags and proceed very cautiously. Sometimes those on the outside can see the whole picture better than you who are standing in the middle of it.

- Seek the Lord first when you believe you are ready to have someone new in your life. If you earnestly pray for his guidance and for wisdom and discernment, he will give you a sense of peace whether you remain single or he brings someone new and wonderful into your life.

- Don't settle for less than what he has for you because of fear that this may be the last relationship you will have. If God wants you to have a new marriage, he has the right partner in mind; and when you come together, you will know that it is right. If you do not have peace, run for the hills.

- Take it slow. Make your relationship with the Lord your first priority, your kids your second, and your dating relationship somewhere down the line. From the beginning in your dating relationships, start praying together, find Christian books to read together, and spend time as a couple with family and friends.

- Once your relationship gets serious, make sure you are spending a lot of time with all the kids. You need to know what real life with these combined families is going to be like before you jump in with both feet.

- Stay accountable to those who love you, and aim to remain sexually pure. I think it may be more difficult for divorced or widowed adults to remain pure than for teenagers because we know exactly what we are missing! Yet God's standards do not change, whether we are sixteen or sixty-five. He will bless your marriage if you stick with the motto "True love waits" (see 1 Cor. 6:18–20).

As soon as newlyweds in a stepfamily cross the threshold, all the "ghosts" of marriages past come in the door with them. If the new relationship has not had time to begin building a firm foundation and strong fortress walls, it may falter when faced with the battering ram pressures of former spouses, combined households, and the care of children.

Solution Suggestions

- Avoid the deception that things will improve after marriage. In dating relationships both people are putting forth their best efforts. If there are habits, behaviors, or activities in your dating partner's life that you can't live with now, don't make the common mistake of thinking that these will get better over time. Chances are they won't.
- Keep in mind that it is only when you feel that you have a whole, complete life with or without a partner in it that you have a healthy life that you are ready to share.
- Remember that God is not a God who forces square pegs into round holes. He knitted you together perfectly in your mother's womb (Ps. 139:13). He seamlessly created all the beauty of the universe. He has not chosen for you a relationship that you have to make fit.
- Allow the children time to get to know your new spouse in nonthreatening situations. Prep them beforehand to

be courteous, but do not expect or demand overwhelming enthusiasm. Give them time to adjust.

- Talk to other stepfamilies and remarried couples about the biggest challenges they face. Be realistic in your expectations for your new marriage and your stepfamily. Establish friendships with those in the same situation, and heed their good advice.

Discussion Questions for Those Planning to Form a Stepfamily

1. How will you spend Christmas? What are your traditions and expectations? How will you work out a holiday schedule with the children and former spouse(s)?
2. How will you blend finances? Which one of you will continue working, or will you both? Will you have one checking account or two? Who will pay the bills each month? Can you afford to marry now, or do you have debt that needs to be whittled away first?
3. In what practical ways will you make your new marriage a priority? Can you commit to such things as daily devotions, a weekly date night, and yearly vacations?
4. Where will you live? Will your new marriage be able to stand up under the strain of living in a home where a former spouse lived, or will you move to a new home for a fresh start, which may cause the kids further upheaval?
5. Do your families accept your dating relationship? Do they welcome stepgrandchildren, or will some of your children be treated differently than others?

6. Do you want to have more children together? Is it a priority for one of you and not the other? If children can't be conceived, do you plan to consider adoption?

7. Do your children need more time before being forced to live with new stepsiblings? What will the sleeping arrangements be for them? Will they need to share a bedroom?

8. Where will you fellowship? Are your spiritual worship "styles" compatible? Will one of you need to change churches or denominations? For example, if one of you comes from a Roman Catholic background and the other from the Assemblies of God, can you find common spiritual ground? Do you agree that tithing is a necessity, or do you give whenever you have extra?

9. Do you get along with each other's friends? Are there friendships that will hinder your relationship with each other? Are there friendships you are willing to set aside for the benefit of your new marriage?

10. After having a lot of time alone as a single parent, how will you work together to ensure that both of you continue to have time for yourselves, time alone to do pleasurable activities that recharge your batteries?

3

The Honeymoon Is Over

Renewing the Romance

> Eat, drink, and remarry.
>
> —Unknown

Brush up on the five love languages: quality time, physical touch, gifts, words of encouragement, and acts of service.

Dear Been There, Done That,

Helppppp!!! I married this great guy/girl with these really great kids. At least I thought they were these really great kids when I met him/her. But now, after only a few months of marriage, they seem to be pulling us apart. Or maybe it's his/her ex-wife/husband that is doing all the pulling. Maybe we are pulling each other. Whatever—the honeymoon's over! It seems like all we do is fight, fight, fight. I want us all to get along, but that seems next to impossible! Can you help?

Sincerely,
Dazed and Confused

Dear Dazed and Confused,

First of all, take a deep breath, pray a big prayer, and have a good cry if you need the release. Better? Now, they're still great kids. You're still a great parent/stepparent. And you're absolutely right! The kids are pulling, the ex-spouse is pulling, and fighting about all of it is way too common in stepfamilies that haven't really jelled yet. You just threw all these ingredients together. Give them time to firm up. Your stepfamily can be a success. Be relieved that you care enough to want it to be a success.

Sincerely,
Been There, Done That

Does this letter sound at all familiar? It certainly does to us. Adam and I were still dating when he and his ex-wife began having disagreements over his visitation with the three daughters we share. When I met him, the girls spent most of their time with him. After we had been dating for several months, their mom remarried, and they began to spend much more time at her house. Because no set visitation schedule was specified, disagreements began to get heated. The conflict spilled over onto the children, who quickly took sides and began to burn with anger. When the disagreement reached an impasse and turned into a legal situation, the pressures mounted on each one of us.

A few months later the court battle continued. Adam and I were now newlyweds with five children at home part-time and at least two children in our home all year except for a few weeks each summer. Two of them were preschoolers. The other three ranged from kindergarten to middle school. While trying to adjust to one another, get kids to school, maintain our jobs, and trudge in and out of the courthouse and our attorney's office, bills, exhaustion, and finally tempers mounted.

We were constantly tired, emotionally and physically. My stepdaughters were like the baby in Solomon's courtroom—being pulled in half. When my husband and his ex-wife had to speak with each other by phone regarding the girls, the tension was so thick and the anger so palpable, it often left us all shouting or in tears.

What Adam and I quickly discovered was that whenever one of our former spouses did something that we thought was unfair or that made us angry, it was all too easy to unleash that anger on each other. After all, the real object of our anger, the former spouse, wasn't physically present to confront. So we redirected our anger at the only target available—each other.

That's when we found the wisdom in the Scripture passage, "In your anger do not sin" (Eph. 4:26). Understanding that verse for the first time brought great relief. It permitted us the freedom to feel angry over the unfairness of the situation, over the heartache and pain. At the

---

We continue to seek any help we can find to remind us that we are not alone in our situation and that others have made it through stronger than when they started.

---

same time, it was a healthy warning of where to draw the line. It was okay for Adam to be angry when he lost time with the girls. It was justifiably, unequivocally, not fair!

It was also okay for me to be angry that my husband was in pain. It was altogether *not* okay for us to do damage to our ex-spouses, our children, our relationship with the Lord, ourselves, or each other in that anger.

We also quickly realized that we would never be able to preserve our fragile new family if we did not preserve our even more fragile new marriage. We began to add tools to our marriage and family toolbox. Communication became a huge priority for us, and even now we talk several times a day in brief interludes about everything from schedules and dinner menus to emotions and long-term dreams.

We read lots of good books, feed on God's Word, and attend parenting classes and marriage seminars. We continue to seek any help we can find to remind us that we are not alone in our situation and that others have made it through stronger than when they started. We believe we have built the best fortress possible together and are determined to hunker down for the long term. We vowed "'til death us do part," and we mean it!

Common Problems to Consider

All new marriages are stressful in the beginning simply because two people are learning to live under the same roof, paying bills, and struggling against selfish natures to put each other first. Second marriages and beyond have the added stressors of children and their complex needs, less time for each other, former spouses who are still in our lives, legal constraints, transportation issues as children go between households, differing discipline styles, and exhaustion that depletes sexual desire and romantic inclinations.

Solution Suggestions

- Figure out a way to have regularly scheduled couple time, and consider it sacred! Gary Ezzo, in the parenting course *Growing Kids God's Way*,[1] recommends setting aside the first fifteen minutes when a spouse arrives home from work as "couch time" for the parents in the home. Teach the kids that no interruptions will be allowed, with the exception of reporting a fire, police at the door, or copious bleeding. If after work doesn't fit in your schedule, set the alarm clock fifteen minutes earlier and have couch time right before everyone gets up each morning.

- Find reliable babysitters as soon as you can. Let the youth pastor at your church know that you need trustworthy teens for babysitting. If you can't afford a babysitter and some of your children are old enough, "hire" them in exchange for extra time to stay up before bed, an extension of their curfew when they go out, or a new clothing item they wanted. If all else fails, find other families willing to co-op babysitting. Put all the kids at their house one night while you go out (which is fun for the kids too), then trade the following weekend so they can have a turn.

- Be spontaneous and exciting. Buy fancy lingerie!

- Don't feel guilty about the time you devote to your marriage instead of the kids. Showing your children what a healthy marital relationship looks like is good for all of you.

- Improve your lovemaking and times of physical intimacy. Sexual release is an important outlet for frustrations that develop in any marriage but especially remarriages. If this is a topic you have difficulty talking about, grab a good book or other resource that can help. Dr. Tim and Beverly LaHaye's classic *The Act of Marriage*[2] provides invaluable information. FamilyLife's *Simply Romantic Nights*[3] gives married couples the chance to open conversational doors and have creative fun while exploring this God-given gift of physical intimacy.

- Don't get in a rut of always going to the movies, watching videos or TV, playing video games, or spending your time on the Internet. These passive activities are not meaningful ways of connecting. Sitting silently in front of any kind of screen does not qualify as "quality time" together.

- Set the timer for fifteen minutes to do nothing but talk, and set the ground rule that conversation can't include talk about the kids.

- Go for a walk or play gin rummy or a board game. Talk about your childhood, your favorite colors, your dream vacation. Get to know each other again.

New stepfamilies have trouble merging—especially bringing together finances and creating contact between new spouses and former spouses. Former spouses frequently remain contentious. Finances of two families coming together can present additional challenges in terms of tax status and deductions, college funds, child support, alimony, and children's expenses.

Solution Suggestions

- Get on a budget if you aren't already on one. Seek help from a financial planner if you cannot set up a budget yourselves. Make sure that at least a little bit of money is set aside for fun couple times and family activities.

- Set limits together of how often you will allow your former spouses to become the topic of conversation between you. Some spouses want to know every detail of your past; some would prefer a general overview.

- Some former spouses intrude into the present through conflict and demands. Erect healthy boundaries to protect your new marriage.

- Don't get into discussions about former spouses or with former spouses when you are tired, angry, or frustrated. Pray about the discussion and politely put it on hold.

Couples who begin second marriages with peace and spiritual preparation can quickly begin second-guessing themselves and God when the bills pile up, the former spouse is on a tirade, appreciation of each other has gone out the window, and the kids are fighting their parents and one another.

Solution Suggestions

- Establish a devotion and prayer time to bring order from chaos. For the first year or two of our marriage, Adam and I prayed together casually but with no routine. I, being the vocal one in our relationship most often, led the way. However, as I grew with the Lord and recognized a deep yearning in my spirit, I realized that being the spiritual leader was *not* my role or responsibility. It was Adam's. I had taken it over, and he had let me. We were out of balance, and it showed in our marriage in many ways. When we began literally getting down on our knees beside our bed each day (okay, most days) and Adam started opening our day with prayer, our marriage truly began to solidify.

- Aim to be each other's recreational partner. As Willard F. Harley recommends in *His Needs, Her Needs: Building an Affair-Proof Marriage*,[4] you want your partner to associate the most fun times in life with you. If he loves golf and you hate it, learn it anyway, or at least go with him sometimes. If she loves to shop and you hate it, go with her sometimes anyway. If you absolutely can't abide the other's top choice for recreation, move down the list and find an activity you both enjoy—then do it as often as you can.

- Develop friendships with other Christian couples. Join a small group at your church or host some "dinners for eight," inviting three other couples to your home for a meal. You will quickly figure out the couple with whom you feel comfortable developing lasting friendships and accountability. Every marriage will face make-it-or-break-it times, and friendships with those grounded in God's Word can help you gain new perspective and "make it."

- Find a church if you don't have one. If you are a Christian who has picked up this book and has been living under the assumption that you can have a full Christian walk and not ever darken the door of a church, you are deceived. With the vast range of musical, worship, and pastoral styles available today, there is bound to be a congregation in your area where you will fit in. If we are all one body of Christ, you are robbing your brothers and sisters of your gifts by not being with them. Even greater still, you are going without the sustenance the rest of the body can give you. Marriages have enough stress from the world every day. Giving them a booster shot of fellowship and worship each week can only make them stronger.

New families can become discouraged when members do not get along. Rebellion in children of remarried couples is common and heart-wrenching. This stress alone can capsize a newly launched remarriage.

Solution Suggestions

- Take advantage of the times some or all of the kids are away to carve out time for yourselves. On Thursday nights, our older girls visit their mom. For several years Thursdays became "our night." Although we still had three children at home, they were young enough to be put to bed a little earlier than usual. Adam and I ordered takeout from a favorite restaurant and curled up in front of a video we rented or read a book aloud together.

- Set goals together for yourselves as a couple, for your children, and for your life. Where do you want to be in one year? Five years? Twenty years? Dreaming together and goal-setting gives you a common purpose and something to look forward to on the tough days.

- Learn each other's love languages. Gary D. Chapman has done an excellent series of love language books that were real eye-openers for me.[5] I am a high-maintenance, type-A, physically passionate, extremely emotional and romantic person. My poor husband! One year into my marriage with Adam, I could not figure out where all those wonderful *feelings* had gone. I knew that he loved me, that I loved him, and that without a doubt our relationship was put together by God. But it just didn't *feel* the same, and I missed it! Then we learned about love languages and how some of our loving actions make the other person *feel* loved, and it was as if someone had turned on a light switch in a dark room. It truly changed my life and marriage.

- Laugh together—a lot. Couples who laugh regularly are more likely to stay together, live longer, and enjoy the life they are living. Read funny stories. Tell each other silly jokes. Enjoy those inside jokes that connect the two of you.

Sidebar—Quick Overview of Love Languages

Love languages are such precious tools in our toolbox and have helped our family so much that I feel the need to share them in more depth here. If you are familiar with love languages, I recommend that you give them another glance. I still need to be reminded daily of our different ways of loving in order to make Adam feel loved with the same passion as the day we married.

"Love languages," in a nutshell, is a term for those loving words and deeds we perform all the time. There are five "categories" of love languages: quality time, acts of service, words of encouragement, gifts, and physical touch. Every human being likes all of these, but one or two will inevitably rise to the top as the ways in which we most often get that head rush, the incredible romantic *feeling* of love.

Do you feel warm all the way to your toes when your partner hands you a box of chocolates, a new tool, or a bouquet of flowers? If so, gifts may be your primary love language.

Does it make you feel best when your loved one gushes about how handsome you are, what a great job you've done, or how much she appreciates that neatly folded pile of laundry? Words of encouragement are your specialty.

Do you feel your heart skip a beat with love when you come home to a clean house, a completed chore that your partner did for you, or some other loving deed? Acts of service make deposits in your "love bank."

When your partner grabs your hand across the car seat or kisses you longingly when you least expect it, and you tingle to the tips of your toes, physical touch is the primary love language you claim.

Can't wait for your loved one to get home? Do you crave those moments when it is just the two of you? Do you feel on top of the world when your partner takes the initiative to set up alone time? Quality time is probably the love language that tops your list.

When a couple begin dating, they cover all of the above five love languages fairly equally. They spend a lot of time together, shower each other with gifts, speak loving words of encouragement, try to outdo each other with acts of service, and love to hug, kiss, and touch. After a relationship gets serious and in the first years of marriage, partners tend to "settle" into showing love mostly in *their own* love languages. After all, if it makes me feel good, it will do the same for you too. Right? Wrong!

This quickly became apparent in our first year of marriage. I am a quality time, gifts, physical touch girl. I could care less if you tell me how beautiful I am (which I wouldn't believe anyway) or if I come home to a spectacularly mowed and landscaped lawn (which I wouldn't notice anyway). My wonderful, loving husband Adam is a words of encouragement and acts of service guy all the way—my last two on the list.

Adam began killing himself doing many domestic chores, keeping the house and lawn beautiful, and cooking for us. (He is a gourmet chef and does 99 percent of the cooking in our home; and yes, ladies, he is almost too good to be true.) He told me how great I looked and how much he loved me. All the while, I was chasing behind him, trying to get him to stop and sit down for a chat with me, wishing he would stop and kiss me more and gaze longingly into my eyes. I left sweet nothings on his pillow, which he knocked on the floor, and I demanded to know what happened to all the greeting cards, silly notes, flowers, and candy I used to get from him, and wondered why we didn't hold hands anymore across the front seat every time we drove.

Adam, meanwhile, longed for me to see everything he was doing, to build him up instead of telling him how much more I needed. He didn't need lipstick prints on his bathroom mirror, nor did he appreciate the new shirts I surprised him with in his closet. He needed a wife who would care enough to run his old shirts to the dry cleaner and wipe down the mirror for him to shave by, definitely two of those no-fun acts of service in my book.

By the end of our first married year, we were both frustrated. What had happened? We were still in love. We were still even loving each other. But we were literally speaking in foreign tongues when it came to loving effectively.

Acts of service and words of encouragement are still more difficult for me, but I try now to stop working before my husband gets home and see the house through his eyes, quickly doing my daily act of service and straightening up the mess that I really don't notice most of the time.

I am still far from perfect in the words of encouragement department—telling him often enough how great he is, how wonderful he is doing, and how much he means to me. As an editor by profession, being critical comes far too naturally (in fact, a fifth-grade vacation Bible school teacher once branded me "Negative Natalie," a moniker I unfortunately often live up to still). I must make the extra, uncomfortable effort to be positive to my husband and children, speaking wonderful words of encouragement to their hungry hearts.

Adam, on the other hand, has learned that he must occasionally remember to drop rose petals on the floor in a trail that leads to a surprise gift in the kitchen (or bedroom). He buys me Cokes when I am focused on working and reaches for my hand often when we are driving together. He tries to balance his tendency to spend his time performing acts of service on our home, cars, lawn, or children with time he devotes just to me.

Discussion Break

Now that you have heard our story, it's your turn. Rank the five love languages below in the order in which you would feel most loved. Ask your spouse to do the same. Compare notes. Are yours the same? No problem. You two can ride off happily into the sunset. The other 99.9 percent of us have to adjust a little—or a lot.

Memorize your partner's top two love languages and speak them often. At first you may have to write down ideas as you think of them and keep the list in front of you in order to love your spouse in his or her language. If you can't come up with ideas, ask your spouse for suggestions after prioritizing your love language lists. It isn't hard to love in a "foreign" language, but it does take conscious effort. And the results are worth it. Spouses with recent deposits in their "love banks" are less cranky, less likely to fight, and more inclined to reciprocate by speaking your language.

His Love Languages	Her Love Languages
____ Quality time	____ Quality time
____ Acts of service	____ Acts of service
____ Words of encouragement	____ Words of encouragement
____ Gifts	____ Gifts
____ Physical touch	____ Physical touch

Ten Quick Ideas for Reviving Romance

1. If the kids are old enough to be left alone, sneak off for breakfast once in a while before they get up.
2. Plan a weekend away, arrange for childcare, and "kidnap" your spouse from work on Friday with the bags already packed and in the car.
3. Go to a theme park or fair without your children and ride the roller coasters or Ferris wheel. Eat corndogs and cotton candy.
4. Play "tag" with H.I.M.I.L.Y. ("Hi. It's Me. I Love You) notes taped in unexpected places. If Adam finds a H.I.M.I.L.Y. from me on a Post-it note on

his steering wheel, for instance, he might respond with a H.I.M.I.L.Y. on my pillow.

5. Choose a song that is "your song," and dance to it. If you already have one, have it playing when your spouse walks in the door.

6. Bring home flowers—just because.

7. Write your partner a love letter recalling all the things that made you fall in love and outlining what you admire most today. Remembering the good old days and focusing on the current positives will help you both keep the fires burning!

8. If you are the partner who never arranges for a babysitter, take the initiative and set up a date. Tell your partner which evening, what time, and how to dress. Hire, pick up, and be prepared to pay the babysitter. Choose your destination for the evening, and let the romance begin.

9. Go swimming or biking, or play a game together. Getting outside of your normal environment or choosing a new or long-forgotten activity can be lots of fun.

10. Make a list of ten or twenty things you've never thought to ask and get to know your mate in a whole new way. Stay away from controversial topics and ask about such things as favorite colors, a best friend's name from childhood, a favorite movie, a dream vacation, and a favorite overall food. Some answers may surprise you.

4

Two-in-One Families

Fitting Everything In

> "Learn to be wise," he said, "and develop good judgment
> and common sense! I cannot overemphasize this point."
>
> —Proverbs 4:5 TLB

If someone had told me twenty-five years ago, when I was twelve, that I would someday be the mother of three and the stepmother of three more, I would have adamantly replied that he was stark, raving mad. I was going to be rich and famous. I was not going to have any children at all. Today I have more children than almost anybody I know.

I continued with the no-kids-for-me mindset right up until I became pregnant unexpectedly with my first child. I was the oldest of four children and had been babysitting my siblings since I was nine. I babysat for our entire neighborhood by the time I was twelve and even helped put myself through college and added to the finances in my first marriage by working in church nurseries and preschools. I knew exactly what having kids was like, and it was not for me.

Words of wisdom: *Never* tell God what you are *not* going to do. He loves to prove you wrong, which is why I now chuckle whenever my teenage stepdaughters tell me they are never going to have kids. Being the mom and stepmom of six was never in my plans. My divorce no doubt was not in God's original plan, yet he was faithful to take my mistakes and mold them into a new life that is so rich, so challenging, and so much better than my plan that it rewards and fulfills me in a way that fame and fortune never would have.

I still have days—many of them—when I yearn for more excitement, adventure, romance, and passion. I long for the day when my husband and I can have our house cleaned, leave the kids home while we run an errand, and return to find our home in the same sparkling, pristine state in which we left it. Instead, it usually looks like a tornado ran right through the middle of it. I get tired of the endless mounds of laundry eight people create and the countless hours I

I was going to be rich and famous. I was not going to have any children at all. Today I have more children than almost anybody I know.

---

spend in the driver's seat of my twelve-passenger van shuttling children to various schools and practices.

I sometimes think the biggest challenge facing stepfamilies is the simple question: How do we fit everything in? The simple answer is: You don't. You fit in what you can, when you can, and you learn to be content with that. You work with what you have instead of moaning about what you don't have. Too many stepfamilies perceive themselves as being handicapped or "less than" a traditional family and hurry to fulfill everyone's smallest desires, running themselves ragged trying to please many, only to find that they

---

Parents in a stepfamily have to make wise decisions over how their precious time together should be spent.

---

are often pleasing none. Tensions build as exhaustion sets in, and bodies are punished by too many fast-food meals on the run.

Stepfamilies, like all busy American families, need to take a hard look at the big picture and determine the very best investments for their limited time together. Some activities are great in and of themselves but will not give the greatest benefit to the whole family unit for the amount of time, energy, and resources they take. A stepfamily's time together is limited not only by the usual constraints of schools, jobs, and extracurricular activities but also by visits to other households. Parents in a stepfamily have to make wise decisions over how their precious time together should be spent.

Common Problems to Consider

Parents who have experienced death of a spouse or divorce often overburden the stepfamily trying to make up for the loss, attempting to give each member everything he or she wants. Children and adults need time simply to be. Each family member needs time at home to experience being together in the new household. Stepfamilies constantly on the go add unnecessary stress to the marriage and family.

Solution Suggestions

- Schedule time just to be home.
- Limit children's activities. Depending on your family size, time constraints, and budget, here are several suggestions:
- Choose one activity for the family per semester or year. In other words, if Susie wants to do karate, everyone in the family can do karate that year. Take turns in different years trying different things. ·
- Choose one extracurricular activity per child per semester or year. If Johnny wants football, fine, but auditioning for the fall play is out. If Brenda wants to be a cheerleader, let her, but she must sit out of the chorus until next year.
- Take a semester or year off of extracurricular activities, and tell the children that the money saved can be added to their savings accounts or put toward a vacation, an air hockey table, a computer, or some other big item that will benefit your family as a whole. Use your "bonus time" to build memories together.
- Allow extracurricular participation during the school year, with the understanding upfront that summer is to be kept open for family time and vacations.

Overcommitted parents and children are exhausted parents and children. Exhaustion leads to crabby tempers, weakened immune systems, and a loss of functionality at school and work. God has called us to strive for excellence in all that we do. We don't honor him by being spread so thin that we can't give our best to anything.

Solution Suggestions

- When you must be on the go at mealtimes, plan ahead. Have sandwiches and salads ready to grab and go instead of having to hit the fast-food restaurants. Invest in a cooler that plugs into your car lighter and keeps foods hot or cold. Pack sandwich bags filled with grapes, baby carrots, granola, and trail mix, and carry juice boxes and bottled water.

- Ask your children what they are willing to "trade" in order to have a certain activity. Are they willing to get up thirty minutes earlier for school and be at the breakfast table on time for a family breakfast and devotions if baseball and cheerleading are going to leave family suppers by the wayside? Are they willing to trade a weekend day or night to help with babysitting younger siblings or housecleaning in exchange for the time it takes you to drive them to practices and games? Will they agree to stay home every other Saturday night for "family night" in exchange for all the evenings they will be away from the family at games or rehearsals? Find a compromise that allows the family to serve the child and the child to contribute to the family.

- If you find that any activities are having more of a negative effect on the whole family than positive, stop them! The world will not end if Bobby has to stop playing baseball in the middle of the season in order to preserve your family's collective sanity. This should be done only in extreme cases, however, as you do want to teach the value of commitment and loyalty to the team.

Couples who commit to too many charities, work functions, volunteer organizations, church committees, and other activities set the example for their children that being busy is more important than being family. Plus, too many commitments can strain the family budget.

Solution Suggestions

- As you bring your children's activities under control, take a hard look at your own commitments. Have you said yes to too many things? Are you willing to make the same exchanges that you are requesting from your children? Ask the Lord which activities should stay and which should go. They might all be good, worthwhile activities, but they might not be the best use of your time. There will always be organizations that need your help, but your kids' childhoods are only a small window of time.
- Find ways to volunteer that include some or all of your family to make the most of your ministry opportunities.
- Involve the kids as much as you can in the planning stages of your activities and your children's, and be strong enough to say no. It is more frustrating to be told no after being strung along with "maybes" and "we'll sees" or to be withdrawn from an activity after starting it than it is to brace yourself and deal with

the disappointment that comes from giving a "no" up front. Just as children are called to obey their parents, remember that parents (and stepparents) are also warned not to exasperate their children: "Don't keep on scolding and nagging your children, making them angry and resentful" (Eph. 6:4 TLB).

Children who get to participate in every activity they desire can develop an inflated sense of their own importance and can begin to focus on self rather than others. Jesus said that we are to be servants. While you, the parents, are undoubtedly serving your children by running them to and fro, the children might be learning to serve no one but themselves. An overcommitted stepfamily develops little unity or sense of family identity.

Solution Suggestions

- Pray and discuss with your spouse, children, and stepchildren which activities they value most and which ones you do. Find the common ground, and seek the Lord's approval. Ask your older children if they truly have the peace of the Holy Spirit that they are being led by the Lord into this activity, not just asking him to tag along.
- Consider keeping televisions, computers, and telephones out of children's bedrooms. It encourages much more family interaction.
- Just as you may have compromised on a recreational activity with your spouse, conduct a family meeting and choose an activity that everyone likes and can do. Are you outdoor lovers? Go on family hikes to

nearby woods or lakes. Prefer the indoors? Choose some board games together and have family game nights. It doesn't matter what the activity is. What matters is that your stepfamily is doing something non-confrontational and fun together.

Families that spend every moment outside of school and sleep time on the go neglect spiritual training. Sports are great; chorus is fine. But if the children in your home are never taught the importance of putting God first, not only by your words but also by your example, they won't.

Solution Suggestions

- Start a family devotion time, and stick to it. When you realize you have strayed off course, get back to it.
- Find a ministry project or way of serving others that your family can do. Our family has found a variety of ways to serve. We have adopted a family in need for Christmas and shopped for every member of that family. We have hosted a family at our former church's Angel Tree Christmas dinner for children who have at least one parent in a correctional facility. Five of us went in the summer of 2003 on a weeklong mission trip to Mexico. Serving others takes the focus off ourselves and whether or not we are getting along and puts it on others and the Lord—right where it should be.
- Make church a priority—for everyone. Whoever is present in the home on Sunday mornings will be present in church on Sunday mornings. Your children

should not need to ask if they are going to church, only what time they are going to church. Remember 1 Timothy 4:8, which states: "Bodily exercise is all right, but spiritual exercise is much more important and is a tonic for all you do. So exercise yourself spiritually and practice being a better Christian, because that will help you not only now in this life, but in the next life too" (TLB).

Discussion Questions

1. Are you asking the Lord each day to order your family's time? Are you teaching all of your children the importance of relying on his guidance for the ways you spend your time? Are you waiting for his answer before going ahead?

2. How many sports, activities, and clubs are your children participating in? Are they playing instruments, auditioning for plays, and joining the honor society? What is taking up your family time after school?

3. How many meals do you eat together as a family—at home—each week? How many meals do you eat together at a sit-down restaurant each week? What can you change to increase these numbers? If you can't make dinnertime work, can you call everyone in for breakfast?

4. Are you nourishing your spirit as well as your body? Is your spouse? Are you feeding your children a healthy spiritual diet? If they are tops in their class and the best players on the teams but die without the saving knowledge of Jesus Christ, have you really done the important part of parenting?

5. Have you or your spouse overextended yourselves by saying yes to too many clubs, organizations, recreational sports, hobbies, volunteer activities, and church functions? In what ways are you willing to allow the Lord to whittle some of these away in order to preserve time for him, for you as a couple, and for your family?

6. Are you doing any ministry projects as a family? If not, how can you find some and get started?

7. What are some activities that all of the members of your stepfamily like to do for fun? What is one recreational activity besides watching TV that you can all do together? If the age range of your children is very broad, you can still take everyone on a walk, go on a bike ride, or take a scenic drive in the car and sing silly songs.

8. Have you ever had a family meeting regarding your activities? Are your children doing activities that they have passion and talent to do, or are they doing the activities that you have a passion for them to do?

9. Can you do a better job of honoring each member of the family by requiring everyone to cheer on the participant at his or her activities? If everyone goes to Jill's play, that is family time. Jill gets to use her talent, and the rest of the family gets to serve her by watching her on stage and being proud of her accomplishment.

10. Are you making the best use of the time you do have? For example, if practices are on Mondays, Wednesdays, and Thursdays and the children scatter to other homes on weekends, are you making it a point to be together every Tuesday, or is everyone still going separate ways to their bedrooms, computers, or TVs? Are you grabbing the opportunity to make Tuesdays family nights and keep them sacred?

Part Two

THE KIDS

5

Dialing Kids Direct

Getting Emotional Long-Distance

"If you would like to make a call, please hang up and try your call again."

—Standard message when a phone is off the hook

Scene One:

The kitchen of a lovely suburban home in a neighborhood near you.

ASHLEY: [*fifteen years old, on the phone with her mother*]
"Mom, you won't believe what the *witch* did now. Dad told me I could go out with my

friends tomorrow night, then *she* came in and told Dad that she thought we were all going to church. Of course, Dad gave in to his *wife*, and now I can't go!" [*voice rising*] "What*ever*! Like she is really a Christian. Like she should have any say over what I can do. She's not my mother."

DAD: [*temper mounting at his daughter's insolence, to Ashley, who is still on the phone with her mother*] "Ashley, you have no right to talk about your stepmother like that. I forgot it was Wednesday tomorrow night, and you know Wednesday night is church night. Now hang up that phone, young lady, and go to your room!"

ASHLEY: [*now ignoring her mother on the other end of the line and screaming at her father*] "What, now I can't even talk to my own mother? You're keeping me from talking to my mommy? [*going back to the phone*] "Mommy, did you hear that? Now he says I can't even talk to you." [*turning back to her father and still not hanging up the phone*] "What*ever*, Dad. Like you guys are not *total* hypocrites!" [*to her mom*] "Mom, I hate him. I hate her. I hate being here. Will you come pick me up?"

Scene Two:

Across the country, in a pretty, old farmhouse with a winding driveway cluttered with bicycles and scooters.

BILLY: [*five years old, tucked lovingly in bed for the night by his mother and stepfather, is sniffling and whimpering, followed by a wail*] "I want my daddy! Daddy!"

STEP-FATHER:	"Well, Billy, I-I'm here, buddy."
BILLY:	[*looking at his stepfather, opening his mouth wide*] "Waaaahhhhh! Not you! I want my daddddddyyyyy!"
MOM:	[*giving the new stepdad a pointed look and rushing to Billy's bedside*] "Billy, you know that you will see your daddy this weekend."
BILLY:	[*now sobbing*] "Wh-wh-when is the w-w-weekend?"
MOM:	"Well, today is Monday, and your dad will pick you up on Friday after school."
BILLY:	[*sniffing loudly*] "How m-m-many d-d-days is that?"
MOM:	"That's four days, Billy."
BILLY:	[*with a loud wail*] "Four days? That's too long. I can't wait that long to see my daddyyy!"
MOM:	[*feeling guilty, looking at the stepdad, who feels defeated*] "I know, Billy. I'm sorry, honey. I'm so, so sorry."

Do these snippets of dialogue break your heart, give you a sick feeling in the pit of your stomach, and cause you the same distress they do me? Variations on these conversational themes are taking place daily in stepfamilies all around us and sometimes in our own. Adults and children in stepfamilies are experiencing emotional long-distance as they begin to live, learn, and attempt to work toward love together. The process is not easy, and sometimes it is excruciatingly painful.

At the beginning of my parental journey, I thought I was placed in the role of parent to rear and teach my children, to help them grow into productive, healthy, God-loving citizens. Instead, my children and stepchildren are helping me grow as much as I am helping them grow. Parenting in a stepfamily is a daily learning experience— and not always a pleasant one.

When single parents find each other and get married again, their wedding day is a joyous occasion. It means the end of carrying the load alone. It means no more lonely nights. It means children will have two parental figures in the home to help rear them. It means someone else can go out at midnight for the gallon of milk that must be in the refrigerator by morning for the breakfast cereal. It means someone else can take a turn with cleanup duty when the eight-year-old is throwing up on his top bunk. It means two people can be chauffeurs to all the sports practices and theater rehearsals. It means intimacy, true love, and a new opportunity for two to become one. It is a precious gift from God, a joyous occasion to celebrate.

Not so much for the kids.

What I did not know when Adam and I got married was that for children involved in a new stepfamily, the wedding day signifies not something they have gained but all that they have lost. They have lost having their single parent all to themselves. They have lost the hope that their secret dream to have their parents back together

---

While parents eagerly look forward to the new family situation, they may find that their children are now stranded across a great emotional divide.

---

again will ever come true. Older children may have lost their position as confidant and friend to the single parent and found themselves relegated back to the role of child. Some of them have lost a home, a school, and old friends because of a geographical move. Many of them have lost their personal space because they must now share a bedroom with another sibling or a new stepsibling.

On top of that, the happy new couple at least had the pleasure of choosing each other. The kids did not get to pick the new stepparent or give their opinion of the stepsiblings who came with the new adult who would now share their home. To the kids, it can be a bum deal all the way around.

The losses that children feel do not mean that the wedding should be called off or that the marriage cannot continue. It simply means that with the joy, there is also pain that needs to be recognized and worked through. While children feel their own losses strongly, they are not far enough down life's path to recognize all the benefits of a stable stepfamily. You can take heart in remembering and emphasizing the many positives of the stepfamily to yourself and your probably pessimistic kids.

As therapist Ron Deal says:

> Stepfamily children, especially those who have lived through a parental divorce, need to witness and learn from a healthy marital relationship. This counteracts the negative and destructive patterns of interaction they witnessed in their parent's previous marriage. . . . Instead of arguments filled with yelling and personal agendas, they watch two people who maintain a win-win attitude negotiate the best solution for their family.[1]

Children with two adults in the home have a bigger safety net surrounding them. When two parents are in the home, they are able to relieve each other, to give one a much-needed break while the other takes over. With two adults around, the children do not have to put on their shoes, grab their things, and hop in the car every time there is a need to run to the corner store. Two adults usually means two drivers to go back and forth to activities, four legs to chase little people, four hands to prepare meals, two mouths to kiss boo-boos, four arms to administer hugs, and four eyes to see everything that is happening in the home.

With a partner for life, moms and dads have an emotional outlet other than their children, which is much healthier for the parent and the kids. Frustrations can be poured into a listening adult's ear before reaching the explosive stage.

Bridging the gap to pull distant children within reach again needs to be a top priority to set a stepfamily on the road to success.

Hurts and heartache can be placed on stronger shoulders than kids can offer.

While parents eagerly look forward to the new family situation, they may find that their children are now stranded across a great emotional divide. Young children may act out or revert to habits long abandoned, like wetting the bed and sucking their thumbs. Tweens, children in the eight- to twelve-year-old range, may either withdraw or cling. School performance may suffer, and parents may begin to despair at the loss of connection with their own kids. Teenagers may head into full-blown rebellion, refusing to respect any authority because they now view ultimate earthly authority, their parents, as having let them down in such a big way.

Whether you are considering joining together as a step-family or have been in the middle of one for years, bridging the gap to pull distant children within reach again needs to be a top priority to set a stepfamily on the road to success.

Common Problems to Consider

Children view a parent's remarriage as a loss, not a gain, and may take it out on their parents and stepparents. Children may deal with a remarriage by acting out at school and at home. Grades may slip, attitudes may go sour, and children may withdraw from physical affection, conversation, and emotional connection with their parent and stepparent.

Solution Suggestions

- Privately let schoolteachers, Girl Scout leaders, and other authorities in your children's lives know about the pressures your children are under and the changes they are experiencing. Ask for grace, mercy, and listening ears. Ask these authorities to let you know if they see trouble spots developing.

- If your children have close relationships with any stable, Christian adults whom you trust, ask the adults to speak into your children's lives. A neutral party is less threatening and can often listen dispassionately and give advice that children can accept without any loyalty conflicts they may feel by opening up to their parent or stepparent.

- Give as much physical affection as your children will allow. Birth parents, especially, should step up the hugs and kisses following divorce and remarriage.

- Stepparents, conversely, should refrain from forcing physical displays of affection on their stepchildren. Be friendly, and give hugs willingly if kids want them. If they are openly hostile or pull away, don't push.

- Remember that each positive interaction, each smile and giggle, each pat on the back that is tolerated or even returned, is a step in the right direction. Hang on to those memories when times are tough and attitudes are out of hand.

- When tempers get heated between any members of a stepfamily, call a time-out and get out of that environment. Arguments between teens and parents can become so hot that violence is just a short distance away. When voices rise and tempers flare, get away from each other. Nothing can be accomplished when emotions are overriding rationality. Exiting through the front or back door can douse the flames of temper almost instantly. (Most people realize they don't want to yell and scream in front of their neighbors.) Approach the issue again only after enough time has passed that both parties are calm.

- If children don't "bounce back" over time, if their grades and attitudes continue to worsen, or if you feel like your relationship has been too damaged to repair by yourself, find good Christian counseling. Children can benefit from individual counseling. Family counseling with the child and parent or with the child, parent, and stepparent can be beneficial to all, as the counselor can help each air his or her views without attacking the others and can give tools, exercises, and instructions for beginning to build a positive relationship.

Stepparents may experience frustration because children who seemed to get along great with them before the wedding ceremony may suddenly begin acting rude and rebellious.

Solution Suggestions

- Require mutual respect for each other, not love. Step-parents and stepchildren cannot manufacture love for each other on the spot. Just as it took time for love to build between you as a couple, so it will take time—probably lots of it—for love to build between step-parents and stepchildren.

- My father has often told me, "Do the best you can with what you've got." Make it your goal to get through that day, that meal, that hour, that visit, with joy. True joy comes from placing **J**esus first, **O**thers second, **Y**ourself last. Many people are Ys; some are even YOs. In a stepfamily, sacrifice is crucial to success. Seek J-O-Y; that's the only way you'll find it.

- Ask the Lord each morning to give you ways that you can make your stepchild's day easier. Remind yourself and your spouse during your daily devotions together

---

True joy comes from placing Jesus first, Others second, Yourself last.

---

what strengths and positives each child gives to the family. That way, when you see only the negatives and misbehavior, you can recall those good points and focus on them.

- Be an encourager of your family. Say things like, "Aren't the Smiths and Joneses a great family?" or "God sure has blessed me with each of you!" Stepchildren may roll their eyes at this, but everyone likes to hear words of praise. Point out all the good things you can find in each member of your family. It will build them up and keep you optimistic about your stepfamily.

Children may not be sure of the rules in this new family. They are unsure of themselves and their role in it.

Solution Suggestions

- Do not allow children to remain holed up in their bedrooms. Instead, encourage and, if necessary, require participation in family activities.
- Make sure that as many meals as possible are eaten together. Go on family walks around the block. If any conversation at all seems to trip over emotional landmines, start with activities that don't require too much verbal interaction, like watching a video together or playing a board game.
- If teens balk at leaving their rooms, exchange "family time" for time with their friends or time alone in their rooms.
- Involve children as much as possible in family decision making and activities. When children are allowed to have input, they begin to take "ownership" of the new family unit. One nonconfrontational example might be to draw up the week's menus and shop for the ingredients together. Assign each child or pair of children a night to make dinner or be the dinner helpers.
- If your family dynamic makes it possible, decide what the basic family rules should be. Give the children an active role in helping decide what consequences should be given for different infractions of the family

rules. For example, teens might suggest that for every fifteen minutes they are out past their curfew, they must come home fifteen minutes earlier the next time they go out. If children help draw up the rules and consequences, they cannot argue when they break them that they did not know what the rules were.

A parent can expect to feel caught in the middle between the children who want their time and attention and the new spouse who expects their loyalty. If only one parent remarries, children may begin to try to avoid visiting the remarried parent. When visits do occur, they may be filled with tension, causing everyone to feel guilty at the sense of relief that accompanies the visit's end.

Solution Suggestions

- Make sure that each child has time alone with his or her parent, especially in the beginning of a marriage. Kids need to know that the new adult in their home is not taking their parent away from them. Even teens who act like they don't want anything to do with their parents need this reassurance. My husband tries to take all of our daughters on "date nights with Dad," where they dress up and go to a nice restaurant just to spend time alone together.
- Keep visits as upbeat as possible while the family adjusts to being together. Aim for "great," but don't plunge into despair if you get "okay" for a while.
- Remember that statistics show that it takes five to seven years for a stepfamily to really start settling. Don't give up during the first two or three.

- Let the stepparent be a fun addition, not the authority, for a while.
- Reassure your children that you will always be there for them. Practice their love languages with gifts, time, words of encouragement, loving touch, and acts of service.
- Pray with and for your children.

Discussion Questions

1. Have you been focusing only on the family unit as a whole? Have individuals gotten lost in the shuffle? How can you arrange your schedules so that parents and their children can have time alone together?
2. Have your kids withdrawn to their rooms, from their friendships, and out of their activities without you noticing or knowing what to do? How can you encourage their participation in the family in fun, nonthreatening ways?
3. How can you engage your children and stepchildren in conversation about what they would like the family unit to look like and what the ground rules should be?
4. How can you bring the Lord into these conversations as the Governor of your home and the deciding factor in how disputes should be settled? Even when tempers flare, children and adults can be reminded that we are called to love and serve one another by God himself, whether we feel like it or not.
5. How can you make required household duties fun? It takes a lot of chores to keep a family running

smoothly. Can you make a game out of them or think of rewards that can be given for jobs done quickly and thoroughly? We have a prize drawer in which I regularly deposit small toys, candy, notebooks, school supplies, jewelry, dollar bills, and other items that all the kids in my family seem to like, regardless of their age. When a task has been done well, schoolwork is complete, or an act of kindness is noted, the children often are rewarded with a chance to choose an item from the prize drawer.

6. How can you design "escape routes" for your children and yourselves when emotions run hot? It is better to have planned beforehand how you will react in heated situations than to try to think rationally in the heat of the moment. Will you go outside, go to your room, or allow your child to run around the block when emotions get out of hand?

7. Can you think of ways to change the environment when tough topics must be discussed with your children? Can family meetings take place at a picnic table at the park where no one can walk out and slam the door of his or her room, casting a pall on the rest? Can you discuss curfews and dating rules with your teen over coffee at the closest Starbucks? He or she would never yell at you in front of the "cool" people there, right?

8. Have you considered professional counseling? Would your child feel comfortable talking regularly with a youth pastor, counselor, or psychologist? What are your health insurance limitations on mental health coverage? Will your church recommend good Christian counselors? (Some churches will even help pay for some sessions for families in crisis.)

9. Are you asking God regularly for creative ways to help you come together? Are you enlisting his help on a daily basis? Keep a prayer journal, and place pictures of each family member in it. List your relationship goals, positive attributes, areas you want to work on, and prayer requests for each one. Use the journal in your daily prayer life. Write down the answers to prayer and the date as a way to remind yourself on tough days that God is moving in mighty ways in your family.

10. Are you still hugging and kissing your children? Did physical displays of affection get lost in the depression and dysfunction of your divorce? Can you often pull your kids into one-armed hugs? Do you still tuck them into bed at night with prayers, no matter how old they are?

An Open Letter to My Stepchildren

Dear kids,

I just wanted to write this letter to let you know that I consider it a great honor and privilege to have been chosen to be part of your lives. I know that we have our difficulties and that having a stepparent was not your first choice. I also know that Romans 8:28 is true. It says, "In all things God works for the good of those who love him, who have been called according to his purpose." That promise means so much to me, because it means that God has plans to make our stepfamily great. It means that God will take even the bad things in our lives and make them turn out okay—even having a stepparent.

I admire all of the special skills and talents God has given you, the way you look after each other, the way you work hard at school, and the way you love your mom and dad. I want you to know that I am not trying to replace your mom or dad, but I am asking the Lord to help me love you like a mom or dad would. He is answering my prayer already! If I can do anything for you, I will try my best. If you need someone to talk to, I will listen. If you can think of things that will make our relationship and family better, I would love your advice.

I know that we will continue to have times when we don't get along, but I want you to know that I want to have the best relationship we can have, a relationship based on respect and honor, not based on my bossing you around and you being expected to obey all my orders. I want to earn your respect with my actions, not just my words.

I love you very much.

Your Stepparent

6

Every Other Weekend and Noon on Christmas

Adjusting to Part-Time Parenting

> Christian or not, whether you intended to or not, when you had your child, you joined with God in creation. *You created with the Creator!*
>
> —Buddy Scott

No one wants to give up time with his or her precious children, but the majority of divorced parents do. Sometimes we miss out on celebrating birthdays, playing Santa Claus on Christmas Eve, and exchanging teeth for money under pillows as the Tooth Fairy. It means that we often have little or no idea what our children are experiencing during the times they are visiting the other parent's home. It means that we lose control over things we have taken for granted their whole lives. It means that virtual strangers to us are often acting out parental roles in our little ones' lives.

As I was starting this chapter, the phone rang. It was my twelve-year-old daughter calling me from her father's cell phone in Oklahoma, thirteen hundred miles from her home with her stepfather and me in Florida. She and her eight-year-old brother were on their annual summer visit, camping and having a big time with their dad and stepmom, their two teenage stepbrothers, and their seven-year-old half-brother. A pang of longing for Jessica and

---

In a stepfamily, even simple phone calls can be a lot to take emotionally!

Joshua, these children I bore from my own body, swept through me so strongly it made me catch my breath at the sound of their voices, so young and innocent. The feeling was followed by joy at their excitement in wanting to include me and the rest of their Florida family in the fun they were having, if only by telephone. The joy was followed by some guilt that I had not thought of them more often in the weeks they had been gone and a niggling of doubt that they could possibly be receiving from their father the same level of loving care that they get the rest of the year from me.

In a stepfamily, even simple phone calls can be a lot to take emotionally!

Because I have had many years of practice at stepparenting, I rose to the occasion. I squelched the longing until I could commiserate later with my husband, reveled in Jessica and Joshua's enthusiasm, put aside the guilt as an attack by the enemy not worth the effort, quickly asked God's forgiveness for doubting my ex-husband, who loves those children dearly, and followed that by a prayerful plea for the kids' protection anyway.

These are just small examples of the heartaches that part-time parenting brings. Part-time parenting is a challenge for parents, stepparents, and the children they share. It comes with differences in parenting styles and inconsistencies in discipline. It creates friction between former spouses and families that may remain steeped in dysfunction. But it doesn't have to be that way.

Stepfamilies can step up to the challenge and overcome the difficulties by getting as many people as possible in the family equation on the same page. Do you have an amicable relationship with your former spouse? With his or her new mate? If so, you are way ahead of the game. Arrange a conference call or face-to-face meeting in a neutral location where the three or four of you can exchange ideas regarding the children's schedules, activities, and ground rules. You will not see eye-to-eye on everything. After all, if you didn't have major differences, you probably would not be divorced. Instead, try to find common ground and come to terms in those areas.

Agree to get "the rest of the story" directly from the other parent (or stepparent) when a child comes to you with a complaint. Inform children that, as much as possible, you will support what their other parent decides in terms of participation in activities, discipline, curfews, and the like. Children who have boundaries that do not shift from home to home are the happiest and most secure children in both homes.

If it is not possible to exchange this kind of parenting information between households, you can at least form consistent boundaries within your own household by getting on the same page with your spouse and children in the home. Establish the policy that everyone follows the house rules in your house, even if the rules are different in their other home.

While you may grieve over the times you miss with your kids, don't allow that grief to continually spill onto them. Watching their parent become sad at every parting creates an enormous load of guilt for children to carry. Save your tears for your spouse's shoulder after the children are out of sight. Do not let the children's absence cast a pall over your home, as this can cause resentment from your spouse and stepchildren. Determine to enjoy life to the fullest while your children are gone and to focus on the positives of less responsibility and more time for yourselves and the other children in your home. Ask the Lord to be your Comforter. He is always faithful!

Common Problems to Consider

Parents who openly grieve over their children's visits to the other home create stress and guilt that make a heavy emotional load for their children to bear. Children are made to feel that they are "abandoning" their parent.

Solution Suggestions

- Keep your grief out of eyesight and earshot. Children should not have to carry their parents' emotional burdens.

- If your grief is overwhelming, get help from a friend who will listen, a family member who cares, or a professional counselor. You must have a full life for yourself, not just rely on your role as a parent for your happiness, in order to be a healthy parent.

- Encourage your children to go and have a good time with their other parent, even if you have to grit your teeth while you do it. Give your children the freedom to love their other parent without guilt from you.

- Find activities to benefit yourself while your children are gone. Developing a hobby, physical fitness program, or Bible study time can only improve your attitude as a person and a parent.

Parents who miss out on once-in-a-lifetime events and special occasions in their children's lives may allow resentment to build against their ex-spouses who seem to be taking the children away from them. Children whose parents do not get along can "play" one off the other.

Solution Suggestions

- Try to establish common parenting ground with your former spouse. Ask if you can come up with boundaries together and if you can agree to ask for more than the child's side of the story.

Keep in mind that you knew you would be giving up time with your children when you divorced. Resenting your former spouse for this loss builds up bitterness that produces really ugly fruit in your life.

- If your former spouse "grounds" a child and asks you to enforce that grounding during your visit, if at all possible, do it. If a child experiences "freedom" from consequences in one parent's home, he or she is likely to resent the one who imposes restrictions.

- Keep in mind that you knew you would be giving up time with your children when you divorced. Resenting your former spouse for this loss builds up bitterness that produces really ugly fruit in your life. Ask God to wrench those roots right out of your heart so that new, healthy emotional growth can begin, but note that this can be a painful process.

Children may feel left out of trips and events that occur with their other family while they are away. They may want to discontinue visits to one parent's house for fear they are missing out on what their other family is doing.

Solution Suggestions

- Try to save really special trips and events for times when the whole family is together. Don't curtail all of your good times by any means, but try not to make kids who are at their other parent's house feel like they are missing out on all the fun.

- Point out to your children that the family in your house will not be getting to experience the fun they will have at their other parent's home. Yes, your children may miss some of the happenings at your house, but they will be having their own fun at their other home.

- Do not allow your child to miss visitation with his parent because he doesn't feel like going, because he is angry at that parent's rules or at his stepparent, or because he wants to do something else. Children who are angry with a parent need time together to work out their problems. Avoidance can create a permanent breach that causes long-term damage.

Large families who abide by the common every-other-weekend visitation schedule find it difficult to fit everyone's choice of activities into two weekends a month. Holiday celebrations must be planned to fit visitation schedules. Longtime traditions must sometimes be set aside.

Solution Suggestions

- If you are extremely frustrated by changes in your traditions, holiday schedules, or family trips because of visitation limits, try hard not to let your children know. Keep negotiations between you and their other parent only, without putting the kids in the middle. Instead of pining for what you can no longer have, create new traditions that belong to your new family.
- Enjoy every minute of what you do have instead of longing for what you must give up. Stepfamilies who are successful are stepfamilies who learn to make the best of their times together. If Christmas needs to be celebrated on December 24 or December 26, is that really a big deal?
- Give each person in the family a turn to choose a family activity for your visits together. It may take

a while to get all the suggestions accomplished, but think of all the fun you will have along the way.

Nonresidential parents find it challenging to be effective parents in just a few days each month or a few weeks each summer. Emotional distance that grows between parent and child when weeks or months go by without face-to-face contact can be difficult to overcome.

Solution Suggestions

- Long-distance and nonresidential (sometimes called non-custodial) parents can keep in touch with kids regularly through email, instant messages, telephone calls, and letters.
- Try to coordinate with the other parent to give the child a cell phone, if appropriate, or a calling card if you are long-distance.
- Send pictures of yourself with your child, pictures of your home, and other "memory builders" to keep your relationship close. Every child likes mail, so letters are a treat!
- Create scrapbooks or photo albums together. Get a second set of the pictures you take during your visits and create one album for your home and one for your child's other home.
- If letter writing is not your thing, buy a tape recorder or video camera and tape messages to your child so he or she can hear your voice or see you. Read books on tape, sing songs, and instill truth.
- Pray for your children every day.

Discussion Questions

1. In what ways have you attempted to parent with your children's other parent? Are you shrewdly undermining the other parent's efforts and giving your children a lack of appropriate boundaries?

2. If you have not been able to establish a friendly, ongoing relationship with your former spouse, are you at least on the same page with each other in terms of parenting styles and house rules so that your children have consistency in discipline?

3. No one can be expected to follow rules he or she doesn't know exist. How have you communicated your expectations clearly to your children?

4. In what ways are you reassuring your children that it is okay for them to go to their other parent's home without worrying about leaving you behind? If you are not, how can you do a better job?

5. If you are not handling your grief and anger well, are you looking for appropriate means to work on this, such as professional counseling or activities to benefit yourself and occupy your time while the children are gone?

6. Are you saving your best times for when you are all together and not subconsciously causing loyalty conflicts in your children by emphasizing all the fun they are missing while they are visiting their other parent?

7. How are you being flexible in regard to holidays and traditions that may be adjusted to fit the new family situation? Can you be unselfish enough to give your children the best of your former family traditions mixed with new ones you want to create?

8. How are you learning to celebrate the times you do have together? What good memories are you building?

9. Are you making the most of your time as a long-distance parent? How are you ensuring that your children know you love them and play a vital role in their lives, even if they are not with you the majority of the time?

10. How are you encouraging your children to gain the benefits of both families rather than dwelling on what they miss or what they had before?

7

Learning to Love
When You Don't Even Like

Falling in Love with All the Children
in Your Home

> I asked him to give me this child, and he has given me
> my request; and now I am giving him to the Lord for as
> long as he lives.
>
> —Hannah, 1 Samuel 1:27–28 TLB

When I married Adam, I was twenty-nine years old; he
was thirty-five. I got thirteen-year-old Lorra, eight-year-
old Leigha, and six-year-old Lydia as part of the second-
marriage package. Adam got four-year-old Jessica and

eighteen-month-old Joshua as part of his. The kids all got a new stepparent and each other. While Adam and I knew God gave us to each other to be man and wife, soul mates for the rest of our lives, we also brought with us to the altar these five children to love, care for, educate, clothe, feed, and protect.

We have never known what it is like to be just a couple. Leigha and Jessica acted as bridesmaids and Lydia as the flower girl in our wedding ceremony. Lorra was my maid of honor. We drove away from our reception with all seven of us in the car that had been decorated with the words "Just Married" in shoe polish. Our wedding night consisted of heading to Adam's house, my new home, putting four younger children to bed, and watching a movie with our teenager, during which Adam fell asleep before Lorra and I

Our wedding night consisted of heading to Adam's house, my new home, putting four younger children to bed, and watching a movie with our teenager.

---

did. A little less than the romantic fairy tale? Sure. But Adam and I were wise enough to know that our children needed to feel like they were part of this new family creation from its very beginning. Not that there is anything wrong with a couple leaving on a honeymoon, but for us, the wedding was change enough for one day.

Our five children, who had seen their original families torn apart only a few years before, needed to be reassured that they had a significant place in this new family we had just created. Even if they weren't sure they loved their new stepfamily, they needed to be shown in a practical way that we were going to act with love toward them. We also recognized that a God who predetermined our days and planned for us to "live the good life" would make sure that we had our equivalent of an exciting wedding night another day.

Despite our united front on our wedding day, the road to relationship in our home has been anything but smooth. Our children demonstrate the effects of their parents' divorces in ways directly related to the age they were when the divorce occurred. Lorra, who was eight when Adam and his former wife filed for divorce and eleven when it was completed, experienced the most heart-wrenching difficulties. Leigha, who was four when the divorce process began and seven when it became final, has dealt with the next biggest batch of anger. Lydia, who was just one year old when the end of the marriage began and four when the death knell sounded, has been the most able to hold her own emotionally.

On my side, Jessica was two-and-a-half when her dad and I filed for divorce and finalized the process. Joshua was not even born. Jessica misses and occasionally pines for her dad in Oklahoma but is happy to have two sets of parents who love her. Joshua, who knows both his father and his stepfather as his daddies, is completely at home in both families.

Justin, our mutual child, has only one set of parents with which to contend and is the happiest of the lot, although he sometimes feels left out of the multiple family equation. When Justin was three and Joshua was telling a story about his two dads, Justin piped up from his car seat, "I have two dads too." An argument between siblings quickly ensued. I gently informed Justin that while Joshua had a dad in Oklahoma and one in Florida, Justin had only one dad. Justin shook his head and quickly replied with a satisfied smile, "I do too have two. I have Daddy, and I have God—my heavenly Father!" We laughed and learned that it is vitally important to all of our children that we recognize and respect all of their familial relationships.

When I was dating Adam, my relationship with my stepdaughters came pretty easily. Their mom at that time visited with them only a few days a month, although in the divorce decree she was given primary residence, Florida's term for "custody." As Adam and I began spending a lot of time together, I fell into the routine of picking the girls up from school, spending evenings with all the children together at Adam's house, even helping to put them to bed. We talked and laughed, shopped a lot, and enjoyed getting to know one another.

On our second date, Adam invited me to go tubing down a Florida river with his girls and some other family members. Halfway down the river, five-year-old Lydia climbed out of her inner tube and into mine, curling up in my lap for her afternoon nap as we floated lazily along.

We had professional pictures of the girls taken as a surprise for their dad for Christmas, spent quality "girl time" shopping, and studied spelling words together. The girls and Adam got to know Jessica and watched baby Joshua take his first steps. It seemed nearly ideal, until visitation conflicts arose and both of the girls' parents decided to remarry. Adam's former wife remarried about six months before Adam and I did. By our first anniversary, my relationship with my stepdaughters had changed—and not for the better.

On the other hand, Lorra, Leigha, and Lydia have been able to bond easily with their stepfather and half-siblings in their mother's home. Jessica and Joshua quickly established a loving bond with their stepfather, Adam, that has never been challenged or threatened, leaving me sometimes resentful that I am viewed at times as the only "bad guy" in the family.

95

Adam and I have had to work hard together to establish ground rules for respecting each member of the family, regardless of our emotions. While I will never be Lorra, Leigha, and Lydia's mother, nor do I want to try to be, I am the mother in the house they share with their dad. In that role, I will treat them as I do the other children in my home. I would not feed everyone else in the house at the dining room table but send my stepchildren to the kitchen. I would not buy new shoes for everyone in the family but them. By the same token, while they do not have to throw their arms around me when they see me, they are expected to be cordial and respectful, and to acknowledge my presence when they come in the door.

Our relationship is not perfect, but it is a work in progress. Because we have been the primary residence for Leigha and Lydia since 1999, and because I work from home, I spend a lot of time with my stepdaughters, who are now teens. We talk about life and love, joke about the movie stars and music they like, and shop together often. We have had to learn firsthand that love is an action verb, not a feeling, and that our commitment to Christianity means that we have to count each other united as sisters in Christ even when we are in conflict as stepmother and stepdaughters. It is confusing and difficult at times. We are learning to say not only "I'm sorry," but also "Will you forgive me?" We have come a long way. We have a long way to go.

Lorra has chosen as an adult not to continue her relationship with her father and me for now, and Adam and I have sobbed on many occasions over her decision. The family all know that I have had nightmares on multiple occasions that one of my stepdaughters is getting married and I am standing outside watching through the windows because I am not allowed inside the church! Leigha and Lydia still cry bitter tears when their ideal of family life butts heads with ours, when they feel like I am the one standing in the way of what they would like to have.

As a stepmother, in order to keep my feelings from being hurt and to keep from holding grudges, I need to have a healthy sense of who I am and what purpose God has for my life. Elizabeth Einstein and Linda Albert share in their workbook *Strengthening Your Stepfamily*, "An effective step-parent shows acceptance. An effective stepparent is open to change. An effective stepparent has a strong sense of personal identity. An effective stepparent believes in children's abilities and allows them to be responsible for themselves."[1]

When we clash as a stepfamily, it feels impossible to love each other. However, God is a Redeemer. Redemption

---

We have had to learn firsthand that love is an action verb, not a feeling, and that our commitment to Christianity means that we have to count each other united as sisters in Christ even when we are in conflict as stepmother and stepdaughters.We have come a long way. We have a long way to go.

---

means that he makes the best of bad situations, turning them around to glorify himself. Regardless of the circumstances, combination of ages, and personalities of your children and stepchildren, you can ask God to intervene and give you love for children whom you may not even like. You can trust that he will. Out of every human being on this earth, he chose you and placed you in these particular children's lives as the best possible parent and stepparent for their individual personalities.

The late Dr. Emily Visher, cofounder of the Stepfamily Association of America and author of *How to Win as a*

Stepfamily, stated in an online article that stepparents play a very special role in the lives of their stepchildren.

> When children have permission to care about all the adults in their lives, it adds richness and variety to their existence. Each adult has something unique to give a child—whether it is a joyful sense of humor, the talent to tell a good bedtime story, or the ability to share the child's delight in visiting the zoo. The more adults contributing to the child's life, the more opportunities the child has to experience diversity.[2]

As you daily sow seeds of God's truth into your stepchildren's lives, God will be faithful. Never stop asking for and expecting miracles in your stepfamily relationship. Settling for mediocre will not produce the abundant life God has planned for you.

Common Problems to Consider

Stepparents may find themselves disillusioned quickly in a new marriage when children who started out as loving angels, as friends, quickly become the enemy after they officially become your stepchildren.

Solution Suggestions

- Don't force the issue. Parents should hold a meeting with their children in which ground rules for behavior toward the stepparent are established. Stress that the goal is respect, not love.
- Stepparents should aim for friendship over authority. While stepparents of young children will probably

act in an authoritative role out of necessity in caring for them, older children should at first, and in some cases always, be corrected by the birth parent.

- Stepparents should establish as much common ground with their stepchildren as they can. If you like to shop, shop together often, just keep an eye on the budget. If you enjoy ice cream, head for the nearest ice cream parlor.

- Build up as many fun, nonconfrontational deposits as you can in your family's learning-to-love bank.

- Keep conversation light and allow the children to lead. Don't try to pull information out of your stepchildren. Let them share at their own pace. Ask about favorite colors and movies, about what they want to be when they grow up, not about what their mom is like or whose house they like better.

- Keep in mind that you can make a difference in your stepchildren's lives regardless of how short your time is with them. Remember the camp counselor that made such a strong impression on you during that one week in eighth grade? Or the first-grade teacher you never saw again but remember with love so clearly? These adults did not have to spend daily, quality time with you for years and years to make a difference. You can love your stepchildren in a way that will impact their lives forever even if it is only on an every-other-weekend or a few-weeks-every-summer basis.

Stepparents may not feel like they "fit in" with their new spouse and his or her children. Children may try to reinforce that notion, dwelling on stories of the past. Stepparents may feel guilty that they are unable to feel the same emotion for their stepchildren that they do for their own children and for their new spouse.

Solution Suggestions

- Try not to take it personally or react negatively when your stepchildren try out stories of your spouse's former girlfriends or boyfriends on you or when they say that they don't like your clothes or that you smell funny. Children have an uncanny knack for pushing buttons that hurt in an effort to test your mettle, size you up, and see where your boundaries are. Laugh at the relationship stories and shrug off the insults. Gently remind them that it is kinder to speak only nice things about people, but don't get your feelings too hurt or allow yourself to respond in kind.

- Establish traditions between you and your stepchildren only. If you like to sew, consider designing costumes together each year or making a quilt. Have stepparent-stepchild nights on the town as well as parent-child date nights.

- Pray often and endlessly that God will give you a soft, tender heart for these children he has placed in your life. This is the best thing I have done in my relationship with my stepchildren. God has heeded my prayers and graciously allowed me to fall in love with each girl, regardless of her attitude toward me. I'm not saying that I never become angry or hurt, but I always love them.

- Remember that God has placed you—out of all the adults on this planet—to be just the right stepparent for these particular children. Let that thought thrill you. He knows that your combination of personality, talents, skills, and strengths is exactly the right fit for this family. He wants you to learn from and grow with these children. He will honor and reward your commitment to them.

Children may put enormous strain on the new marriage by ostracizing stepparents and treating them disrespectfully. Many kids are downright rebellious and rude. A stepparent may become angry with the new spouse when the spouse doesn't come to his or her defense when the stepchildren attack. A parent may feel that the stepparent is overly sensitive or too harsh on the kids.

Solution Suggestions

- Remember the tortoise in Aesop's fable? If you are experiencing frustration, slow and steady wins the race. Stepfamilies need time to get the right mix. Don't expect a perfectly baked cake the moment you throw the ingredients together!
- Teach your children the five love languages and have them rank theirs. Share with them what your love languages and their parent's are. Actively aim to love each child in his or her language. Note that love languages for children may be different with different people. For example, while a daughter may rank quality time as her top choice with her dad, she may want gifts from her stepmother and siblings.
- Establish ways that the stepparent can be the "good guy." For instance, you be the one to hand out weekly allowances.

- Think before you give an automatic no. Although parents are quick to say no when doing something for a child may prove inconvenient, saying yes may bring a child joy. For example, playing in the hose outside might make muddy feet and wet clothes, but it also puts smiles on young children's faces. Play in the hose with them if you really want to make a memory.

Children may become angry at the new stepfamily because their other parent is enraged about the new marriage and hates the new stepparent.

Solution Suggestions

- Remind your stepchildren that you are not trying to take their mother or father's place, but that you would like to develop a relationship with them that feels comfortable for all of you.
- Never malign or insult your stepchildren's mother or father, even if their parent is horrible to you.
- If the other parent is hostile and you feel you must address the issue, address it with your spouse or with the parent, not through the children. A stepparent, especially a stepmother, will *never* improve her position by pointing out any flaw in the children's mother. In fact, pointing out the mom's hostility most likely will backfire and make the child defensive.
- Encourage your stepfamily often. This may be very difficult for a stepparent who is maligned or rejected by stepchildren. *Do it anyway.* Focus on every positive

you can think of in the children, and verbalize it. As you begin to share good things with your stepchildren, not only will they feel better about themselves, but you will begin believing and focusing on those good things you speak.

- Remember that you are the adult and they are just children—even if they are big children who are old enough to know better. You set the example—always—regardless of their bad behavior. Bad behavior is never an excuse for more bad behavior.

- Remember that these are not your children. They are God's children, his unique creations, just as you are. You are just one of the facilitators he is using to bring to fruition their potential to live for his glory. Let that fact lift the pressure of perfection right off your shoulders.

- Stepchildren should also be reminded that God has put this family unit together to be uniquely joined for a reason that will bring glory to him. When they act with love, even when they don't feel it, they are honoring God as well as their parent and stepparent.

- Use visual aids, if necessary, to explain to children how obedience and respect for authority, even their stepparents, pays off for them. Draw two adults forming a human "umbrella," with the children underneath. List common problems "raining" down on that umbrella, such as bills, worry, conflict, and danger. Explain to the children that when they remain obedient and under the authority, their parent and stepparent can protect them from the things in life they are not ready to have to bear.

Discussion Questions

1. How am I letting my children know that by honoring their stepparent—especially when they do not feel like it—they are honoring God?

2. Am I asking God to give me the desire to love my stepchildren in exactly the ways they need most? Am I complaining to him or thanking him for this opportunity to sow into their lives?

3. How am I encouraging my stepchildren on a regular basis? In what ways am I demonstrating that they are special to me?

4. What do I expect from my stepchildren? Am I aiming to make their lives easier or expecting them to make mine easier?

5. Have I learned my stepchildren's love languages? What specific things have I done in the last week to love them in their top two love languages?

6. What am I doing about my hurt feelings when my stepchildren do not treat me well? What healthy outlets am I using, such as prayer, time for myself, and fun activities, so that seeds of bitterness never take root?

7. How often am I examining my own heart and asking for my stepchildren's forgiveness for the ways that I fail them? How can I enlist their help to make our relationship better?

8. In what ways am I putting myself—consciously or subconsciously—between my spouse and my stepchildren? Am I creating any loyalty conflicts between my mate and his or her children?

9. How generous can I be both with giving time to my stepchildren and with allowing them to have time

with their parent, my spouse, without me? What activities am I enjoying with my stepchildren, and how can we create fun times and traditions together? What special things can we enjoy without anyone else?

10. What can I do to build relationship with grown stepchildren? Have I invited them to lunch, written them letters at college, asked them to help me shop for their parent's birthday, or tried other creative ideas to keep communication lines open?

Twenty Ideas for Stepparent-Stepchild Fun Times

1. Assemble a kite or model rocket together and fly it at a local park or beach.
2. Read a book aloud together.
3. (Girls) Get makeovers together and take "glamour" photos of each other.
4. Go fishing.
5. (Girls) Talk about boys. Casually impart healthy guidelines while giggling over infatuations and relationships.
6. (Guys) Talk about girls. Impart healthy guidelines while opening up about past infatuations and relationships.
7. Show your stepchildren your childhood home.
8. Drive your stepchildren by their former home—but only if this will instill a sense of nostalgia, not reopen old wounds.
9. Get a kitten or puppy to take care of together.
10. Bake something sweet together, and enjoy it with a favorite movie.

11. Go to the gym together.
12. Exchange stories of when you were little. They weren't there for your childhood, and you were not there for some of theirs.
13. Find a Barnes & Noble, Borders, Starbucks, or other coffee shop and share conversation over a smoothie or cappuccino. For younger children, an ice cream shop will do instead.
14. Play "I Spy," "Twenty Questions," and sing favorite songs in the car.
15. Look through photo albums together of when your stepchildren were little. Allow them to share memories of their former family.
16. Look through photo albums of when you and your spouse were little.
17. Play a favorite board game, or put together a puzzle.
18. If your stepchild's grades are good, it is your visitation time, and the school gives permission, surprise your stepchild with a "skip day" and go to the mall, the game room, or the movies.
19. Take your stepchild to work and then out for a "power lunch."
20. Build a scrapbook together of new memories.

8

The Divided Highway of Discipline

Who Does It, When, Where, and How?

> Young man, do not resent it when God chastens and corrects you, for his punishment is proof of his love. Just as a father punishes a son he delights in to make him better, so the Lord corrects you.
>
> —Proverbs 3:11–12 TLB

Dear Honey,

When we got married, I thought you said we were going to share everything. We do share our time, our money, and our love; but often I feel like we do not really share the most important thing we have—our children. It seems like every time they act up for me, you throw your hands up and say that you are not getting in the middle of it.

When I think the kids are running out of control, you think I am being too hard on them. When I say no, you wait until I turn my head and then say yes. I feel like I am always the bad guy, having to restore some order to the chaos created by overindulgence. You probably think I am rigid and no fun, which is what everyone else in this family thinks.

We are a house divided against itself, and I am afraid we might not be able to remain standing in the long run. How can we get on the same page before we tear this family apart?

I love you.

Love,

Your Wife, the Wicked Stepmother

While I never actually wrote this letter to Adam, we have had many conversations along this same theme. Discipline in stepfamilies is tricky, the difficulty compounded by the former spouse who is the other parent in the family unit. Most of the fights that Adam and I have had in our married life have been over the children—the children and their problems, not getting to see the children, the children and their activities, the children and how they are treating us, the children and their loyalty to another family, the children, the children, the children. Of course, having six of them makes the problem seem even larger.

When Adam and I met, some of our children were so little that it was natural for both of us to assume an authoritative role in their lives right from the start. Joshua was an infant, and Jessica was a preschooler. Their father was more than a thousand miles away, so it was easy for them to accept

---

Discipline in stepfamilies is tricky, the difficulty compounded by the former spouse who is the other parent in the family unit.

Adam unconditionally in the role of dad. Lydia and Leigha were in elementary school, and Lorra was in eighth grade. For my younger stepdaughters, it was not shocking that I expected them to eat the food that I prepared, told them to brush their teeth before bed, or asked them to go clean their rooms. Having been taught basic Christian values, they knew that obeying adults was the right thing to do; and for the most part, they did.

In my ignorance and eagerness to please, I did not know that I was jumping into the role of mother too fast for my stepdaughters'—and especially their mother's—comfort. One thing Adam and I did not do in the beginning of our relationship was set boundaries around how involved I would be in the care and discipline of Lorra, Leigha, and Lydia. Adam was happy to share the load, and I wanted to show him how much I could help him by sharing it. While I did share a lot of nonconfrontational, fun times with my stepdaughters-to-be, I also had high expectations from the get-go. They were the kids; I was the adult. When they were with me, they would listen to me and follow my instructions. End of story.

While the girls did obey me for the most part, I learned much later that they didn't like it. I also learned that their mother, especially, did not appreciate it, and this compounded the girls' difficulties. It is only years later in my role as stepmother that I am realizing how much I took on too soon and how much slower I should have gone. Extenuating circumstances made it easy for me to convince myself that I had to do these things for the girls or no one would; but in reality,

I insinuated myself into the role of acting like a mother to them far sooner than I should have.

Family psychologist Dr. James H. Bray and John Kelly, in their book *Stepfamilies: Love, Marriage, and Parenting in the First Decade,* chronicled data from a nine-year study of one hundred stepfamilies and one hundred nuclear families. They discovered that the two critical issues of early stepfamily life are figuring out the balance of parenting and stepparenting.

> The family has to develop a method for integrating the stepparent into the family. It is also best to limit the stepparent's role during the early period of stepfamily life. A stepparent needs to develop a relationship with his stepchild before he tries to start parenting that child.... *The bottom line is they have to agree on how to deal with the child.*[1]

As our kids got older, they "wised up" to the fact that they could plead the "She's not my mother" case and attempt to get out from under my requests. Adam and I have had to learn—often the hard way—to make sure that we are tiptoeing around the fine line that separates our children's strong parental loyalty from their ability to comply with the directives I give.

Adam has to play the disciplinarian more often now, a role that is uncomfortable for him with his easygoing, nonconfrontational nature. And I have to back off—way off—and trust him to run the show, an extremely uncomfortable position for highly driven, control-freak me. We have learned that we have to prepare ahead of time and behind the scenes for what will come at us next so that we don't lose control of our emotions.

Despite my many mistakes, God is faithful. One big turning point in our family came when Adam and I learned that we first had to come to an agreement behind closed doors or over the telephone before any of our children could receive a yes to a request that took up family time or resources. We don't always remember to follow this guideline, and chaos almost always ensues. We are still learning to say, "Let me check with your father first," or "Let me check with Natalie to see what the plans are for the rest of the family before I give you an answer" before we give blanket approval to teenage plans.

We discovered that even young children quickly become experts at figuring out which adult will give them what they want—and try to push for an answer from that parent before the two adults in the home get a chance to put their heads together. We have had to draw a firm line and teach our kids that if they push for an answer or try to go to the other adult in the home after one adult has said, "We'll see; let me check on our plans," the answer is an automatic no. Only this firm boundary preserves the family from many instances of frustration.

For example, let's say that hypothetical teenage stepsiblings Joanne and Shannon agreed to help their family one Sunday by watching their younger siblings after church so the parents in the home could go out for lunch. After church, Joanne ran up to her mother and asked if she could go eat pizza with her friends. At the same time, Shannon hit up her father for ten dollars to go to the movies with her friends. Each parent thought the other teen would be home to watch the younger children. Now both teens are happily on their merry way, and the parents are pointing fingers at each other for allowing Joanne and Shannon to get out from under their commitment.

This scenario happens in families who are not stepfamilies too; but families who have not experienced the losses of death or divorce are often better equipped emotionally to deal with it. In stepfamilies, the pressure is greater to feel a sense of unity, making disharmony difficult to take. Terri Blackstock, a wonderful fiction author and friend of mine who also has a stepfamily, told me once that stepparents are more likely to administer the law to their stepchildren, while a parent extends grace. I think Terri is absolutely right. The stepparent feels like the teen got off easy, while the parent believes the stepparent is taking too harsh a stance. This leaves the parents pitted against each other while the kids shake their heads in dismay at the adults' bad behavior or leave the adults to their fighting and go do whatever it was they wanted to do in the first place.

For stepfamilies embarking on a new life together or those who have been at this game for a while, there are always new tools we can add to our family toolboxes to help us run in top shape. One of the first things we did as a couple was to enroll in our church's sixteen-week parenting course, *Growing Kids God's Way*, by Gary and Ann Marie Ezzo. This gave us an opportunity each week to feel like we were doing something positive directly related to our family's well-being. We learned biblically based reasons for parenting methods we chose and practical tips for creative discipline. We attended popular Christian author and youth leader Angela Elwell Hunt's workshop titled "Ten Things Children of Divorce Want You to Know but Will Never Tell You" and enrolled some of our children in Gary Sprague's well-known *Kids Hope* divorce recovery seminar.

We were proactive in seeking out information, education, and other resources to help us achieve realistic expectations. Even when the information we heard was not new to us, much of it was encouraging and affirming in that many of the things we were already doing naturally were the right things to do, according to the experts. If we walked away with even one new insight, practical tip, or feeling of hope, we considered the time and money well spent.

Growing Kids God's Way or any biblically based parenting book or course can give you a starting point for conversation about discipline in your home. It can give you the opportunity to quiz each other about the homes you grew up in, your parents' methods of discipline, and your own parenting styles and preferred discipline methods. More important, it gives you the chance to discuss these issues when you are not already in the middle of a child problem that requires your attention. It can help you sift through the best of each of your preferred methods and come to terms with what you each see as your role in disciplining your collective children.

From the sources we used, we learned to teach our infant, who had a horror-movie, high-pitched scream, how to use sign language to communicate with us before he could talk. We saved our sanity and the children from spankings on many occasions by the simple utilization of the "interrupt rule." When your children need to speak, they may place a hand on your arm or shoulder and stand quietly until you can turn to them. The parent's job is to place a hand on the child's hand to recognize the child's need to speak while finishing the conversation in progress with whomever the parent is speaking, whether in person or on the phone. We taught the children to "appeal" when they were inadvertently given conflicting orders from each of us. We learned each other's love languages and tried to focus on creative ways to correct our children. We also learned that we had

113

to keep our children's personalities and learning styles in mind when giving orders and expecting obedience.

For example, one child in our home is independent, a natural leader, and resents direct orders. She obeys much better when her "help" is enlisted, rather than when we tell her what she must do. Another daughter is very logical and analytical but has difficulty processing too much information orally. If

---

By focusing together on learning styles, personalities, and discipline, parents in a stepfamily home feel like players on the same team, pulling together for a family victory.

---

we want that child to do four or five things in the morning before she leaves for school, a written list with these items on it works wonders. She loves to check them off as they are accomplished. If the list is given orally, inevitably two or three things are forgotten, creating frustration for all of us.

By focusing together on learning styles, personalities, and discipline, parents in a stepfamily home feel like players on the same team, pulling together for a family victory. By becoming proactive rather than reactive, negative emotions have a less likely chance of rearing their ugly heads. Stepfamilies who purposely work together to integrate the stepparent and delineate discipline duties are stepfamilies with a much higher chance for success.

Common Problems to Consider

In an effort to please their spouses, stepparents jump into the role of disciplinarian before they have established a positive relationship with their stepchildren. Parents extend grace and mercy, while a stepparent is more likely to administer the law.

Solution Suggestions

- As a stepparent, don't assume that your spouse wants you to discipline your stepchildren. If you administer the law, it may cause a backlash from the former spouse and may cause a rift in your budding relationship with your stepchildren.

- Ask the Lord to show you if you are being overly critical, sensitive, or negative in regard to your stepchildren. Solomon asked for wisdom, received it, and became the wealthiest and most powerful man on earth.

- Find ways to have children comply without giving direct orders. For example, post a list of family chores with family members assigned to each chore. Make sure parents and stepparents are on the list so that everyone in the family is working together as a team. Hand kids a list of their assignments that they can check off and present for a word of encouragement or reward when done quickly and thoroughly.

- Avoid comparisons of the child's two families. When a child tries the "We don't do it that way at Mommy's house" tactic, matter-of-factly state that Mommy may do things differently, but this is the way we do it at Dad's house.

Parents of stepfamilies do not make the effort to equip themselves together for parenting by utilizing good books, workshops, parenting courses, and other resources.

Solution Suggestions

- Find tools for your family toolbox. Attend workshops and parenting classes, and read good books. Ask your mate how the two of you can handle disciplinary issues in a balanced way.

- Discover your children's learning styles, and consider their personalities as you parent. If giving verbal orders is a constant frustration with one child, try giving him a written list. Instead of squaring off against strong-willed children by giving direct orders, give them a choice of two chores, for example.

- Reward children as much as you can, using positive reinforcement for good behavior rather than relying on negative consequences for poor behavior. For example, straight As on a report card in our home earns the student a monetary bonus.

Children learn to "work" their parent against the stepparent to get what they want.

Solution Suggestions

- Just as two parents would, present a united front to the children in your home. Let them know from the start that getting a no answer from one adult in the home does not mean they can try to get a different answer from the other. Inform them that playing one adult off the other is grounds for an automatic no the next time they want something.

- If you disagree with your spouse's method of handling the children or a decision he or she has made, never challenge your spouse in front of the children. Take him or her aside, go to your bedroom, or head out back, and discuss the issue away from little ears.

- As the birth parent, even if you disagree with your spouse, do not overrule him or her. Every time you do, it sends children the signal that they do not have to heed what their stepparent says, because you will undo it for them anyway. Either allow your spouse's word to stand and put up with your child's objections, or confer privately with your spouse and ask him or her to back down. The adult who gave an order or a no answer is the only one who can rescind it if his or her authority is to remain intact.

- Keep laying your divorce and your misdeeds of the past before God. Only when you have experienced the freedom of accepting his forgiveness can you parent without guilt over your past. Guilt often leads to lenient parenting, which can cause children to become self-centered and overindulged.

- Begin praying for each child's future spouse on a daily basis.

Stepfamilies enter their union with unrealistic expectations that they will bond easily and present a united front. Although stepfamilies can chart a smooth course over the years and benefit each other greatly, they will never be a "nuclear family."

Solution Suggestions

- According to Bray and Kelly, conflict and disagreement are a normal part of early stepfamily life. Everyone feels stressed.[2] Expect tension and build in healthy ways to relax.

- Be proactive as parents, brainstorming possible scenarios before they occur—from toddlers having temper tantrums to teens breaking curfew. Decide now how you will handle them. If you have already pictured going down that road, you are better equipped to stay calm during the crisis. Preplanning ways to handle conflict takes away the potential for clashing when crises do come.

- When your children and stepchildren disagree with decisions you are making, remind them that Romans 8:28 is true: "In all things God works for the good of those who love him, who have been called according to his purpose." If they believe that verse and trust in the Lord, he will make good come out of all decisions parents and stepparents make—good and bad. He will also bless the children and stepchildren for honoring and obeying their parents' and stepparents' authority, even though they did not like it.

Too many couples fail to decide together before being put to the test what methods of discipline will be used in their home and who will administer them. This causes one parent to become too strict and the other too lax, or allows discipline to fall by the wayside, causing children to grow up without firm boundaries.

Solution Suggestions

- Have parents bear the greatest burden of discipline in the early years of your stepfamily. Give the stepparent a chance to integrate before thrusting him or her into the unpopular role of disciplinarian.
- Get creative in your correction. In former television actress Lisa Whelchel's parenting book *Creative Correction*,[3] she advocates many nontraditional

methods for getting your children's attention when they are misbehaving. For example, Whelchel's family has a rule that no screaming is allowed inside their home. When this rule is broken, the one who has lost self-control must go outside until he or she has regained self-control.

- Decide together if you are in favor of spankings. If the parent is not, the stepparent should never cross this line with his or her stepchildren. If the children will not behave for you, turn them over to their parent for discipline and take a time-out to regroup. If one parent does not want to use spankings, ask that parent what methods of discipline should be used.

- Be consistent in discipline, no matter how hard it feels. Let your yes be yes and your no be no. Children who learn that pushing can sometimes wear you down will push harder every time.

Discussion Questions

1. Are my spouse and I in agreement concerning the ways we discipline the children, or is this an area of constant friction? If it is causing us to falter as a couple, how can we work to get on the same page?

2. What creative ways of correction have we instituted to help our family run smoothly? Are there other methods we could also employ?

3. How are we encouraging our children and rewarding them for what they do right instead of focusing on what they do wrong?

4. Are we balanced in our discipline approach, or is one parent carrying all the burden of discipline? Do our kids see one of us as the "easy" one or "good guy," while the other one is always the heavy? If we are out of balance, how can we fix this?

5. In what ways are we gaining our children's compliance without giving direct orders, such as chore lists and reminder emails? Do these work better than verbally demanding obedience?

6. What tools have we placed in our family toolbox? What workshops, parenting classes, or other resources could we use to help us refine our skills?

7. Is the stepparent in our home doing too much of the discipline without enough relationship building? Do we need to rethink our disciplinary patterns?

8. How are we remaining consistent in our boundaries and discipline? Are our children experts at wearing us down until we give in? If so, how can we work to stop this damaging behavior?

9. If one adult in the home thinks the disciplinary methods are not working, how can we lay aside our loyalties to our children, keep from getting angry, and find a way to compromise?

10. How are we networking and developing friendships with other stepfamilies and nuclear families to observe how their families work together? Do we have friends or family we trust for good parenting advice?

9

New Kids on the Block

Brothers and Sisters, Unite!

> The Top Three Reasons for Sibling Conflict:
> You have more than one child.
> Your children live in the same house.
> Your children's living-together skills are still
>   developing.
>
> —Dr. Todd Cartmell

The woman had brought with her into the house two daughters, who were beautiful and fair of face, but vile and black of heart. Now began a bad time for the poor stepchild.

"Is the stupid goose to sit in the parlor with us?" they said. "He who wants to eat bread must earn it. Out with the kitchen-wench."

They took her pretty clothes away from her, put an old grey bedgown on her, and gave her wooden shoes.

"Just look at the proud princess, how decked out she is," they cried and laughed, and led her into the kitchen. There she had to do hard work from morning till night, get up before daybreak, carry water, light fires, cook and wash. Besides this, the [step]sisters did her every imaginable injury—they mocked her and emptied her peas and lentils into the ashes, so that she was forced to sit and pick them out again. In the evening when she had worked till she was weary, she had no bed to go to but had to sleep by the hearth in the cinders. And as on that account she always looked dusty and dirty, they called her Cinderella.

—From the story of *Cinderella*
by the Brothers Grimm

Stepparents and stepsiblings have long had bad reputations and difficult times commingling, if you believe the fairy tales. Cinderella's stepsisters teased her mercilessly, worked her fingers to the bone, and generally treated her like dirt. In many stepfamilies, children brought together by marriage into stepfamilies think this is the way they must behave in real life too.

In our home, Lorra, Leigha, and Lydia had to share their dad when we got married with not only another girl but also a cute baby boy, Joshua, the first son to come into Adam's life. Then came Justin, shaving off yet another slice of the parental pie. Jessica and Joshua suddenly had to share their time with their mommy with the three older girls. Natural sibling rivalry multiplies in stepfamilies, where parents are prizes to be fought over and personal possessions must be protected from the "outsiders."

This mind-set, however, like the type of treatment Cinderella received from her stepsisters—even though she one-upped them in the end by marrying the prince—is abso-

---

Natural sibling rivalry multiplies in stepfamilies, where parents are prizes to be fought over and personal possessions must be protected from the "outsiders."

---

lutely antithetical to our Christian walk. It is self-centered and "me"-oriented. If Jesus said we must love our neighbor as ourselves, it follows that those in our own family—even a stepfamily—must rank even higher on our love list.

Nice theory, right? But how do you make it a reality? In an interview I did in 2002 with Word recording artist Sandi Patty, the mom and stepmom of eight children, Sandi shared that the initial rule in her stepfamily was that the kids did not have to like each other, just honor each other and treat each other with the courtesy and respect they would any other person they were just getting to know. This kept the kids from having to try to make themselves feel emotions that they didn't feel and allowed them the opportunity to develop friendships on their own, at their own pace.

In our family, Jessica and Lydia, who are exactly eighteen months apart in age, had to share a bedroom for a time after we got married until we moved to a bigger house in 2002. Their personalities are very different, but close proximity helped them develop a bond of friendship that enabled them to work and play together. Today they are either thick as thieves when no one else is around, or they are squabbling like normal adolescent sisters do.

All of our younger children look up to their older stepsisters, and their stepsisters treat them with some affection

123

or casual disdain, depending on the day. What we have done to foster stepsibling bonds, not rivalries, is to make sure we spend as much time together as a family as we can. Stepsiblings will never form any kind of relationship if they don't spend time together. Make your family times fun, and no one will grumble too much about participating. Go bowling. Have a backwards dinner (wear your clothes backwards and eat dinner starting with dessert first). Be creative.

The second thing we have done to promote family harmony is to give the stepsiblings time away from each other. While they are required to participate with good attitudes in family activities, they are also permitted to have their own friends and interests, as well as time with their siblings, their parent, or even just their stepparent. This allows each child to be the center of the parent's attention sometimes, and at other times gives him or her practice at interacting with a variety of ages and personalities.

We have chosen as a family to keep the only television and family telephone in the great room, the only common room in our two-story home. We do not have Internet in the children's rooms, and we also allow no food or drinks in the bedrooms. With these guidelines, kids are forced to come out of their rooms and interact with other family members in order to use the phone, watch a show, check their email, or eat a snack. These guidelines also limit our children's temptation to become deceptive, whether it is teens making plans with friends behind our backs or smaller children eating too much candy in their beds.

When siblings initially refuse to have anything to do with each other, allow them time and space. Parents and stepparents have so much riding on their fantasy of what their stepfamily should be like that they can impede the progress of their stepfamily in reality. Ask God to give you patience in the area of growing your children's relationships with each other and with you.

Common Problems to Consider

Stepsiblings do not appreciate the fact that there are new children sharing their parent, their space, or their possessions. Stepsiblings may feel that the time, energy, and money their parents used to invest in them may now be given to the new siblings.

Solution Suggestions

- Reassure your children often that adding new family members did not diminish their life. Let them know you love them now more than ever. Assure them that they will not be deprived of anything by the new family members.
- If the children's attitudes cross the line from uncertain and anxious to downright selfish and mean, remind them that we are to put others before ourselves. Teach them that, as God looks after the little sparrows, he is still looking after them. And you are too.
- Each parent can take his or her stepchildren aside separately and allow them to air their grievances about their stepsiblings, as long as they are not tattling. (Tattling is telling how someone else has wronged you

---

Refrain from intervening in ordinary stepsibling quarrels. Let them work it out with each other. Remember that siblings fight too.

---

with the motivation of getting them in trouble.) Airing grievances allows children to express their own hurt over being offended. Listen to their hearts with compassion, no matter how trivial their complaints may seem. By listening to your stepchildren's side, you help them to feel less like you are always jumping to your own children's defense.

- Ensure that each child in the family, even an infrequent visitor, has his or her own space somewhere in the home. When children are at their other family home, do not allow their stepsiblings to use their things without permission.

Parents and stepparents can be overprotective and step in too soon when stepsiblings do not get along instead of letting the kids work out their differences.

Solution Suggestions

- Refrain from intervening in ordinary stepsibling quarrels. Let them work it out with each other. Remember that siblings fight too.
- By the same token, if any stepsibling is verbally or physically abusing any child in your home, intervene immediately.
- Establish firm ground rules that only words of encouragement will be spoken in your home. Allow the children to point out to you when you speak negatively.
- If anyone in your home tends to act like a bully, take time to read Frank Peretti's *The Wounded Spirit*.[1] It is a great reminder that God wants the beautiful, popular, and strong to protect the plain, unpopular, and weak.

This book is also available in an audio version and video curriculum.

- Teach your children healthy conflict resolution. Many relationships are never repaired because the people involved don't have the tools to fix them. Show children healthy ways of letting off steam, such as going for a walk, agreeing to disagree, agreeing to formulate solutions after tempers have cooled, and humbling themselves to apologize.

- Parents should be the example in apologizing when needed. Saying a simple "I'm sorry" is acceptable when a mistake or injury is accidental. Humbling yourself enough to ask "Will you forgive me?" when you have hurt someone purposely—especially in anger—is a must. Express often and openly that you are sorry when you hurt someone and ask for forgiveness from those you have wronged.

- Teach your children to do "right for right's sake." Each person is accountable to God for his or her own behavior, regardless of what the other person does. Show your children how to "clean out their hearts" by asking for God's forgiveness as well as their offended brother's.

Some stepfamilies fail to start out with a positive plan. They need to be determined to create a family identity, in small increments, over a long period of time.

Solution Suggestions

- Eat meals together. If conversation is awkward or heated, find a family devotional or other short reading that can be a good conversation starter.

- Play "high, low" around the dinner table. Have each family state one "high" (positive thing) that happened during their day and one "low."
- Require each member of the family to honor each other, not be gushy with emotion. Use common courtesies like "please" and "thank you."
- Have a family storytelling time during which each of you shares childhood memories. When stepsiblings get to know each other's past and develop empathy for each other, they are much more likely to eventually find commonalities and become friends.

Parents who want to make up for their children's losses caused by divorce may favor them over their stepchildren, fostering jealousy between stepsiblings.

Solution Suggestions

- As parents, make things as fair as possible for all of the children in your home. Giving ten gifts to one child and two to another does not promote friendly relations.
- Assign chores evenly and rotate them so that one child is not always stuck doing the same job.
- Model friendship by working to remain best friends with your spouse, and make sure that your family spends time with other families who have good relationships.

Because stepfamilies are dealing with so many issues from the moment the parents exchange "I do's," children experience high levels of stress, which may make it difficult

for them to focus on establishing new friendships, even
with those now living in the same home. Stepsiblings'
personalities also may clash, just as your personality clashes
with those of some people you know. You may love them in
Christ but feel like you don't have much in common.

Solution Suggestions

- Don't expect too much from your kids at first. Just as they need time to warm up to their new stepparent, give them time to warm up to each other.
- Find activities your stepsiblings have in common, and do them.
- If stepsibling clashes are seriously disrupting the family, point to the truth of God's Word instead of pointing fingers. If God says that we are to love all people, to count others as better than ourselves, and to love one another as our highest calling, stepsiblings should be expected to live that out with each other just as with anyone else.
- Have stepsiblings in your home build or create something together. They could paint a room, cook dinner together, sew a quilt, or build a bookshelf. Find something they can accomplish together. Be enthusiastic about their end result.
- If stepsiblings have reached a relationship impasse, agree to become a mediator in reaching a compromise. Have the first child state his main complaint directly to the other child. Have that child repeat what he heard, rather than coming to his own defense or airing his grievance in return. Tell the first child to talk about how he feels, not focus on blame for

what the other child allegedly did. Do not allow the other child to interrupt. After one child has aired his hurt, repeat the process with the other child. Ask the children what they think they could do to make it better.

- When insults have been exchanged among stepchildren, require them to include one nice thing they can say about each other as they are apologizing.

- If the stepsiblings reach some compromises, consider having them draw up a contract that each child signs. Make copies for each child, and keep the original. Once a child has committed to a certain behavior in writing, there is a better chance he or she will stick to it when reminded of his or her end of the bargain.

- If stepsiblings must share a bedroom and your budget allows, permit the pair to redecorate any way they want to—as long as they agree on the décor together. If they paint the walls a garish green or hideous hue of purple but learn to like each other while doing it, which is more important in the long run for your family?

- When your children work together well, celebrate it! Break out the ice cream, praise them verbally, and encourage them to keep working together.

Discussion Questions

1. How are we modeling and teaching healthy conflict resolution to our children? Have we learned to humble ourselves and go beyond saying "I'm sorry" to "Will you forgive me?"

2. In what ways have we given each child physical space to feel at home in our house so that he or she does not feel threatened or out of place when he or she visits? How are we respecting our children's possessions and space?

3. Are we requiring stepsiblings to respect each other's space and possessions?

4. What are the biggest points of contention between the stepsiblings in our home? Have we really listened to their complaints? If we notice a common theme, how can we address it without being preachy?

5. Are we jumping in to save the day too often for the stepsiblings in our home? If we are constantly in the role of mediator, how can we step back and let them work out their own issues?

6. On the other hand, are we encouraging our children and stepchildren to air their grievances to us when they have reached a real impasse? Are we truly listening and helping facilitate a solution between the children, or are we dismissing complaints with a lecture?

7. What interests do our children have in common? How can we foster that bond between them?

8. In what ways are we drawing our family together by holding devotion time, family outings, and the like? What new things can we try?

9. How are we planting biblical truth in our children's hearts in regard to their relationships, not just with us and each other, but with the world?

10. What are we asking God to do in the hearts of our children? Have we enlisted his help in bringing our children together?

Part Three

THE FORMER
SPOUSE

10

Turning Fury into Forgiveness

Divorce Didn't Make Them Go Away

> Hatred stirs old quarrels, but love overlooks insults.
> —Proverbs 10:12 TLB

When two people divorce, they usually experience a great sense of failure as well as anger, sorrow, and grief. Some time after the divorce, however, a sense of relief and an underlying sense of hope often begin to emerge. Hope arises for a future healthy relationship, even another marriage someday. Even if a person has guilt over past failure, he or she is still likely to desire to start fresh again someday.

If two divorced people had no children together, when they finally go their separate ways there can be a final curtain on the relationship, a closure, an ending. When two people with children divorce, they expect closure, but the reality is that the former spouse does not go away, and the relationship, in some form, continues to exist. You both will be your children's parents, and except in extreme cases, you both will be in their lives all of their lives—like it or not.

The former spouse is constantly present in your children's appearance, expressions, and mannerisms, in their memories, in the hope that lives in them that you will get back together again someday, at their activities, in the reality of shifting them back and forth for visitation, and in the fact that some type of communication must be maintained in order to finish parenting these children that you started together. Thus, at some point in the midst of your desire for something fresh and new, you realize that divorce did not mean the end like you thought it would.

Christians whose marriages end in divorce find themselves in the midst of great emotional contradiction. Bitter feelings almost always accompany the ending of a union that was supposed to last a lifetime; but as a believer in Christ, you are called to love even your former spouse—the one person who caused you such tremendous pain that you can barely tolerate it. Even in this heart-wrenching situation, Jesus knows exactly how you feel. He knows that kind of pain personally. If you think it is hard for you, think of Jesus loving Judas after that kiss of betrayal in the garden. With Philippians 4:13 tucked firmly in your mind and by repeating it like a mantra—"I can do everything through him who gives me strength. I can do everything through him who gives me strength. I can do . . ."—you can form a positive, even loving relationship with your former spouse one day.

It isn't easy. It isn't usually fast. Old wounds take time to heal, and Jesus is the only one who can keep those wounds from turning into thick scar tissue instead of healthy new growth. If you are willing to turn your whole life—past, present, and future—over to the Lord and give him back the steering wheel, he will drive you to a place of beauty, rest, and complete healing. His healing is so thorough that your mind can probe even the memories from your former

---

Bitter feelings almost always accompany the ending of a union that was supposed to last a lifetime; but as a believer in Christ, you are called to love even your former spouse.

---

marriage that should be the most excruciatingly painful, and the pain will no longer be there at all. I know from personal experience that you can still remember what happened, see the events, but the emotion is no longer attached. It is like watching a movie of someone else's life; it doesn't feel like it really happened to you. Hallelujah! And all the divorced people said, "Amen."

If you are not in that place yet, I am sure that sounds like a television shopping network deal—too good to be true. I assure you it is not. God has promised in his Word that he wants to give you life and give it to you abundantly (John 10:10). He will be true to his Word if you will allow him the opportunity to weed out the old bitterness and heartache and sow new seeds of love. For some this is a tough trade-off. To get rid of the heartache and bitterness means they also have to lay down their right to revenge, their right to complain, and their right to continue to try to punish the former spouse who wronged them. But it is more than a fair trade. If you give up your rights and God heals your pain, you will no longer care about what would have been fair and will want only his desires for you.

Your relationship with your former spouse will improve, and your children will be more stable and happier for it. They do not care if what happened in your marriage was fair nearly as much as they care about seeing their family,

---

If you can't seem to let go of anger and forgive, ask God to work in your heart. He will.

---

even their divorced family, get along. When you act with love toward someone who caused you pain and dysfunction, you are demonstrating selflessness. You are demonstrating that you love your children more than you love the fight. You are demonstrating Christ.

Common Problems to Consider

Guilt, resentment, bitterness, and anger accompany divorce, and they don't go away just because a judge finalized the end of the marriage. Some former spouses carry these negative emotions for the rest of their lives.

Solution Suggestions

- If you have never learned to literally get on your knees by the side of your bed and pour out your pain to the Lord, I can offer no better suggestion than to start today. If you can't seem to let go of anger and forgive, ask God to work in your heart. He will.
- Trade revenge for rest, "fair" for the freedom that comes with laying down the burden of anger. Don't worry, your former spouse will someday stand before

the Lord and give an accounting of life, just as you will. No one who hurts another person ever really gets away with it.

- If you do not want to forgive your former spouse, ask God for the desire to want to be able to forgive. Try saying out loud, "I forgive you," while envisioning your former spouse. Over time this can be very freeing.

Negative emotions have a far greater effect on the person having them than on the target of the bitterness. Unmanaged anger and roots of resentment can cause physical pain and a sick spirit. Anger and unwillingness to forgive block us from a close relationship with God, who calls us to love and forgive, regardless of who has "trespassed against us." Bitterness causes cynicism to develop along with a deep-rooted distrust. It can quickly change a formerly optimistic person into a pessimist.

Solution Suggestions

- Do everything within your power to resolve hard feelings and tough issues between you and your former spouse, then back off. You cannot control the other side of the equation.
- Seek the Lord's guidance, receive wise counsel, take every step with prayer, and put your children's best interests ahead of your own. That is all you can be expected to do. The Lord will work in your heart and

Negative emotions have a far greater effect on the person having them than on the target of the bitterness.

in the situation even if you do not immediately get the results you want.

- Ask the Lord for a softening of your spirit. Ask friends and family members if they sense a negative attitude or hardening of heart within you. Find an accountability partner with whom you can share your hurt and anger, pray about it, and let it go.

Anger and resentment toward a former spouse who is not physically present get unloaded on whoever is present, meaning that kids and the new spouse get caught in the crossfire. When one parent in the home is angry, the rest of the family's attitudes tend to follow suit. Children who grow up with an angry parent are more likely to carry anger into their own future relationships.

Solution Suggestions

- Decide every day to lay your anger at the Lord's feet. Ask him to show you any small ways you can honor your former spouse for God's and your children's sake.
- If you and your former spouse cannot seem to get on consistent friendly terms no matter how hard you try, don't force the issue. Give your ex-spouse space at games and school events, and give your children the freedom to move freely between their two parents. If you take your children to a basketball game and they want to sit across the gymnasium with their father, let them go with your blessing. The less they feel pulled, the better, even if you sometimes feel the sacrifice.
- Refer to your former spouse as "your mom" or "your dad" to your children, not the more formal "mother"

and "father." Children sense your disdain when you formalize their other parent's title. "Your mom called; she wants you to call her," is much friendlier than, "Your *mother* called. She wants you to call her back."

- If the situation remains hostile to the point that you begin to see definite damage to your children, seek outside help for them and for you. Ask your pastor or close friends for recommendations of a good, Christian counselor who specializes in stepfamilies and in your special circumstances, whether it is hostile teenagers, mental illness, alienation of one parent by the other—whatever your special case may be. A good counselor can help you define healthy boundaries and forge improved relationships with your children, as well as be a neutral sounding board and source of advice.

A former spouse, especially one who has not remarried, may still expect you to meet his or her needs, wants, or demands. Your ex-spouse must not dominate your new marriage. A former spouse may want to use you as his or her "sounding board" or "rescuer" or may want to revisit old arguments.

Solution Suggestions

- Limit your contact with your ex-spouse. Make sure that your conversations center on the children and issues that concern them. Do not let your conversation disintegrate into a rehashing of your marital mistakes every time you talk.
- Make sure that you are not leaving your new spouse in the lurch to help your former spouse. Once you

have taken vows in a new marriage, your attention and energies must remain focused there. Your former spouse can call AAA for a flat tire, find a new friend to talk to, hire a handyman to fix the toilet, or get the cat down from the tree without you.

- Never hide information from your new spouse about phone calls and visits by your old spouse. Jealousy is all too common in second marriages, but love does not envy. Head it off at the pass by not giving your new spouse any reason to worry. Have your telephone conversations with your former spouse where your new spouse can hear.

Harboring negative emotions and being unwilling to forgive prevents closure of the former relationship and deadening of the pain. It keeps you tied, however unwillingly, to the one you divorced because the negative emotions are a constant reminder of that person and broken relationship.

Solution Suggestions

- Journal your path to emotional healing. Write down the impressions you receive during your prayer time. Acknowledge on paper the moments of peace and joy that begin to come.

- Revisit your journal to see your progress and to find peace on days that are filled with turmoil. Seeing the ways God has worked in your life written down will encourage you on days when you have trouble sensing his presence.

- If contact or phone conversations start getting ugly, decide ahead of time how you will handle them without becoming angry. My husband and I often anticipate conversations with our former spouses and dialogue the possible outcomes and our responses before we get on the phone.

- Do not hang up on your former spouse; it is not honoring to him or her as your children's parent.

- On the other hand, you do not need to listen to verbal abuse or allow things to become hostile. Let your ex-spouse know that you want to work toward positive relations and that you will talk again once you have both regained composure.

- Be faithful to return phone calls from your former spouse (within your personal boundaries). Do not promise to call back if you are not going to call. If you do promise, make the call.

- Just as you expect members of your own household to honor each other with common courtesies, so you must honor your former spouse with the same. Remember the "magic words" from childhood. "Please" and "thank you" can go a long way.

- Begin to act with love even if you do not feel it. If you know your former spouse has only one car, offer to transport the children both ways. Your former spouse may not deserve it, but acts of kindness will show your children that you act what you believe. Acts of kindness can also go a long way to restoring peace between you as coparents.

- Treating your former spouse badly just because he or she treats you that way is no excuse. You are called to do right for right's sake, regardless of what anyone else is doing.

Discussion Questions

1. What relationship did you envision with your former spouse once your divorce was finalized? What actually occurred? Have you been able to progress toward a working relationship?

2. If conversations with your former spouse start to become confrontations filled with anger and accusations, how can you maintain your calm? In what ways are you able to diffuse heated emotions?

3. How are you keeping the tension and anger between you and your former spouse away from your children? Are you allowing them to heal by trying to heal the breach between you and your former spouse?

4. If a confrontation occurs in front of your children, in what ways are you reassuring them? How are you demonstrating to them that angry confrontations are not godly, correct behavior?

5. Have you reached the point of being able to apologize to your children and to your former spouse in times of conflict, even if your former spouse never apologizes in return?

6. Have you put closure on your former marriage with your ex-spouse by refusing to rehash it in conversation again and again? Are you keeping your contact focused only on the children you share and their present needs? If not, how can you develop the self-control not to go down "Bad Memory Lane"?

7. Are you spending time in your prayer life asking God to heal your hurt, diffuse your disgust, free you from frustration, and lift you into a new kind of love relationship with your former spouse—not a romantic love, but the same sincere love we are to show all of

humankind? How are you praying about your relationship with your ex-spouse? Are you asking God to fix him or her or telling the Lord that you will do whatever he wants you to do in every situation?

8. If your ex-spouse continues to cause trouble, angering you at every turn, are you guarding your heart against seeds of frustration turning into roots of bitterness? When you begin to slander your former spouse or speak sarcastically or cynically about your former spouse or marriage, these are warning signals that bitterness has crept in.

9. What are you sowing into your own life in order to continually weed out any seeds of resentment? What books are you reading? To whom are you turning for godly counsel? If you are unsuccessfully trying to sort out your feelings on your own, what steps can you take immediately to find someone you can trust to help your family through the emotional upheaval?

10. In what ways have you established clear boundaries around the role you will play in your former spouse's life? If you are constantly being called in to rescue or are in the role of a sympathetic ear, is this causing conflict in your new marriage? How can you work toward a relationship that focuses on your children?

11

Joint Custody, Joint Decisions

A dry crust eaten in peace is better than steak every day along with argument and strife.

—Proverbs 17:1 TLB

Scenario No. 1

Johnny's parents divorce when he is seven years old. For the next eleven years, Johnny is subjected to constant warfare between the two people he loves most. Every time his parents speak on the phone, they yell insults. His mother usually ends up in tears. Johnny's mother tells him constantly what a liar his father is and that he doesn't care about them.

Johnny begins to resent his father for the pain his mother is experiencing. He is torn between protecting his mother and wishing she would stop expecting him to be her confidant and comforter. By his teenage years, Johnny is angry and defiant. He wants nothing more than to get away from both of his parents. He is determined never to marry.

Scenario No. 2

Katie's mom and dad divorce when she is seven years old. Her mother so resents her father for his affair that she makes it difficult for Katie to spend time with him. She continuously solicits Katie's sympathy by telling her how terribly her father hurt her, how unfair it was that he left them. She puts so many conditions and restrictions around Katie's father's attempts to spend time with his daughter that he finally pretty much gives up.

Now Katie's dad has a new wife and two new kids. Katie gets phone calls from them a few times a year and presents on her birthday and Christmas, and she spends a couple of weeks each summer at her dad's new home. She feels like a stranger there. By her teen years, Katie feels ugly and unlovable. She dresses older than her age and flirts with older men. She gives her body to men who like her in an attempt to find the love she needed from her father. It is very likely that she will go through a divorce herself someday.

Scenario No. 3

Megan's mom and dad divorce when she is seven years old. Although they are both hurt and angry, they work hard to keep those feelings away from their daughter's eyes and ears. They agree that no matter what happened between the two of them, Megan is worth the effort to be civil and work together to coparent. They give up their right to revenge.

When Megan's parents remarry, Megan gets the benefit of four parents in her life, and the four adults agree to uphold each other's boundaries as much as possible. When Megan is mad at her mom and calls her dad to vent, he listens to her but does not encourage her anger toward her mom. Instead, he also asks to speak to her mother to get a complete picture of what is happening in their home. He tells Megan she must obey her mom even when she doesn't feel like it, and that God will honor her obedience even if it turns out that her mom was wrong.

Megan's mom, the custodial parent, encourages Megan to spend time with her dad and makes sure to keep him informed of their daughter's school events, extracurricular activities, and medical appointments. While these parents do not agree on many things, they always make it a priority to think about how their actions will affect Megan.

Megan grows into a teen who respects her parents and stepparents in both households. She is determined to marry the man God has for her and not to follow in her parents' footsteps, but she recognizes the good example her parents have set for her in difficult circumstances.

Which of the above scenarios most applies to your household? Which scenario do you want for your children? The obvious choice for all of us, I hope, is number 3. I don't think any parent purposely sets out to place children in the middle of conflict or wants his or her children's pain to continue long after the divorce is final. However, after divorce, it is too easy to make children messengers, sympathizers, and outlets for your pain. Do not do it! It will absolutely, unequivocally destroy your precious children. It will destroy their love for one or both parents, their trust in people and often in the Lord, and their self-esteem. They can become permanently emotionally damaged and continue the curse of a dysfunctional family into the next generation.

A Christian singer who experienced divorce told me in an interview recently that at the height of the difficult divorce proceedings with her ex-husband, the two of them made it their goal that by the time their oldest child graduates from high school, they want to be able to sit down around a table with their extended families, share a meal together, and celebrate their oldest child and his accomplishments. At times when they still do not see eye-to-eye, keeping that ultimate goal in mind keeps them focused on finding common ground and reaching a compromise. They remember that storing up anger and resentment will prevent this goal from ever becoming reality and will rob them—and their child—of that precious memory together.

If your divorce was ugly, working together as parents after the divorce is probably the biggest challenge you will face. It is harder than remarrying and more challenging than the separation and divorce in the first place. Parents must work very hard to face their bitter feelings and leave them in the past in order to head into the future with an attitude toward compromise and successful coparenting. Letting go of the desire for revenge, or at least justice, especially for a party who has been wronged by adultery, neglect, or abuse, may feel like a sacrifice, but revenge is never sweet when we exact it ourselves. Let God handle it, and give your anger to him to diffuse.

Family experts all agree that the best thing a parent can do—out of all the good things that can be done for children—is love the other parent. Yikes! That is a tall order after divorce, but it remains the truth. The children who clear the hurdle of their parents' divorce with the fewest scars, bumps,

> If your divorce was ugly, working together as parents
> after the divorce is probably the biggest challenge you
> will face.

and bruises are the ones whose parents work together with good attitudes for them. Parents who handle post-divorce coparenting right expect their children to respect their other parent and stepparents. They exchange information freely and participate jointly in activities and extracurricular events so that a child does not have to choose which parent can come to which occasion. They encourage and continue contact with extended family, such as grandparents, aunts, uncles, and cousins. Their children experience the gain of new family members but never the loss of former family members being exiled from their lives.

Mission impossible? Never say never. God is still in the business of miracles today, and he can make your pain and anger dissolve through prayer and supplication. He can help you put away your past as the husband or wife of your former spouse and help you go forward as coparent with that person. If you ever had a screaming match with your ex-spouse in front of your children before, during, or after the divorce, do you remember the looks on your children's faces? Did they freeze in fear, cower and cry, or explode with anger? Do you remember the guilt and pain you felt when you saw those precious faces? Do you ever want them to experience that again? If you can visualize your children's pain when you have conflict with their parent, it is a great incentive for keeping your coparenting on an even keel.

No matter what your former spouse did to you in your marriage, if he or she is not a physical or sexual threat to your children, you must put your children's need to have a healthy, strong bond with that parent ahead of your own compelling need for justice. In fact, you need to actively promote their relationship with that parent. This may be the most important thing to grasp within these pages, and it undoubtedly is one of the most difficult things to do. Even if your lifestyles are different, your moral standards at opposite ends of the spectrum, your religious beliefs on different pages, your children need both their dad and their mom in their lives. Get used to it, and get on with it.

If the other parent has not only left you but also left the children, provide for your children healthy outlets with Christian adults. Encourage your spouse, the stepparent, to befriend your child with extra activities for the two of them. Do not try to force a parental bond. And as a stepparent, do not be discouraged if you get a lot of resentment at first. It may not be your fault that their parent is gone, but you are the available target for their hurt and frustration. It may not be fair, but you are the adult. You can take it with grace and provide a healthy example of true love for your stepchild.

In addition to the stepparent, or if the child refuses to bond with the stepparent, is there a strong uncle, grandfather, or family friend who can step in and mentor your child if his or her father is gone? If mom is out of the picture, is there a loving babysitter, grandmother, or someone

---

Your children need both their dad and their mom in their lives. Get used to it, and get on with it.

---

at church who can befriend your child? Encourage your children to talk about their feelings toward their absent parent, and teach them to have their own daily devotional time and to journal. Remind them that God is also their parent and loves them unconditionally.

If you are a parent who finds a former spouse to be so vindictive that it is difficult for you to spend time with your child, take the pain and don't give up. Your children need you, and they need to know that you divorced their other parent, not them. Make every effort to continue to have a strong, positive bond with your children in whatever ways you can, even if their other parent makes it a grueling challenge. No child deserves to be abandoned.

Common Problems to Consider

Parents who encourage their children's anger toward their other parent create angry children. Once anger is instilled, it does not limit itself to the other parent. Parents who hate their former spouse, who clearly let their feelings of hurt and disgust show in front of their children, teach their children to hate. Once hatred takes root, it is lethal to all of their relationships.

Solution Suggestions

- If your former spouse is hostile in front of the children, grin and bear it. Count to ten, excuse yourself to take a walk, politely say you will call back later. Use every ounce of self-control you can muster. Not only will you be a good witness to your children, but also to your former spouse.
- When you keep your cool, you demonstrate healthy conflict resolution to your children instead of fueling their anger by attacking their other parent.

- When anger responds in kind, the flames only get higher. A gentle answer turns away wrath (Prov. 15:1). I know of one situation in which a stepparent was being insulted and berated by a birth parent, and the stepparent began repeating, "I love you with the love of the Lord." This statement so flabbergasted the angry parent that the parent hung up and did not call back!

- Look up Scriptures on anger and hatred and examine their characteristics and results with your children. Then look up passages on self-control, kindness, and love. Memorize some of these verses together, or write them on cards and place them around your home as good reminders of the way we are to treat one another.

- Remember that you used to love your former spouse and that your children still do. You created those beautiful children together, whether you want to remember that part now or not. In order to have healthy self-esteem, your children need to know that they are products of love. By treating their other parent harshly, you are tearing them apart.

- Once relations cool down and reach a tentative friendly stage and you are absolutely certain there will be no ugliness in front of the children, try a get-together with all of your children's extended family. Plan a birthday party together at a local park or pizza parlor. Some families even visit each other's homes, opening Christmas presents together or having an Easter egg hunt.

Parents who refuse to share information with the other parent and teach children to be close-mouthed are teaching their children to be deceptive. Children who are taught to hide information from a parent become sneaky children in other areas as well. This is especially pronounced in their teen years.

Solution Suggestions

- Refusing to share information causes misunderstandings in stepfamilies. If friendly relations with your ex-spouse are a reality, suggest a meeting between you and your spouse plus your ex-spouse and his or her new partner. Pick a neutral location like a nice restaurant where emotions are not likely to get out of control, and strategize ways to keep your kids from playing both sides against the middle.

- Break the ice by getting to know each other. Discuss each of your visions for your children and the role their stepparents will play. Agree ahead of time to change the subject or end the evening if the conversation begins to get heated. It is better to make a little bit of progress and stop there than to attempt too much and end up in a worse position than you started.

- If a meeting with your former spouse would not be welcomed but there is not outright hostility, ask if you can sit down next to your child's other family at a school program or ball game. Get used to making small talk and coordinating schedules during these times of nonconflict.

- If your former spouse is particularly close-mouthed and private, do not try to pry information from your children about their other household unless you believe that there is something truly harmful or dangerous going on there. Some parents simply do not want children to share any information with their other family. If asking the simple question, "What did you do this weekend at your mom's?" causes your child to look like a deer caught in headlights, give him or her a way out. Tell your child that lying is never acceptable, but that he or she can respond, "I'd rather not say" or "I've been asked not to tell you that."

- If you are moving, getting a new phone number, or going on a trip, inform your former spouse in a timely manner and with the proper information. Do not tell your children to hide this information from their other parent. Children who have to hide things experience high levels of guilt and stress. Their guilt often turns to anger or apathy.

Parents who are openly hostile and refuse to see or speak to each other place the burden of communication on their children's shoulders, a burden too heavy for them to carry. They were not created to be messengers. They also learn to relay only information that would be beneficial for them and thus sometimes create more conflict when messages are not passed on in full or in a timely manner.

Solution Suggestions

- If you need to discuss an incident at school or need to switch visitation days, do not pass these messages through the children. Refusing to speak directly with the other parent elevates the child to a position of false authority. It also increases the likelihood of miscommunication, which creates more conflict. You are the adult; act like it. Communicate directly to your former spouse when it comes to dealing with your children.

- If emotions still run too high and you are afraid the children will experience tension if both their parents are in the same room, take turns attending events for a while but still communicate directly by phone.

- If your former spouse refuses to communicate in person or by phone, you can always send information through the mail or email. Print the emails you send, and keep a copy in your files. If your former spouse claims not to have received any of your letters, send them by certified mail with a return receipt. It costs more, but the letters must be signed for on delivery, and you get the delivery receipt back.

- Without placing the burden of the decision on the kids, ask your children if it is easier for them to have you both present at field trips and soccer games, or if they are more relaxed when it is only one of you at a time. You both may have been knocking yourselves out to attend every activity of your child's, only to find that he would really prefer to have his dad at his soccer games and his mom at violin recitals. Neither parent should have to miss out on special events, but seeing your former spouse at every baseball practice and game five times a week may cause too much stress for you, your ex-spouse, and your children. Constantly keep seeking the right balance for your family.

Parents who cannot lay their anger aside and work toward the best interests of their children are self-centered parents who are wreaking havoc on themselves and their children far more than on their former spouse. Anger is self-centered, and it is also self-defeating. If you both love your children, keep that, not the past, as your focus.

Solution Suggestions

- Remember that your goal with your former spouse is not to become best friends, but to be friendly enough that children do not experience conflict each time the two families run into each other.
- Create a future goal, such as getting together for high school graduation, to work toward. Keep that goal in mind whenever disagreements arise.
- Constantly work to find middle ground. If you want to give your daughter permission to date at sixteen and your ex-wife does not believe in traditional dating at all, instead of having two standards, find the compromise. Find out what your ex-wife does believe in, and work toward common ground. Perhaps it is just your definition of dating that differs, and what you both mean is that you would be comfortable allowing your daughter to date at sixteen if she always goes out with a group of friends or if she has her date attend family activities. Rather than polarizing each issue, aim for the middle.

Parents who deny their children a healthy relationship with their other parent and their stepparent create children who feel like they were not good enough for the other parent's love. They are much more likely to have low self-esteem and trouble in relationships than those who are free to love both parents and stepparents without guilt.

Solution Suggestions

- Do not equate your children's time and relationship with their other parent with money. You cannot deny your former spouse visitation with the kids because child support has not been paid. This may be a situation that makes you extremely angry, but you have no business handling it in front of your children. Take whatever legal measures you have to, but keep your mouth shut in front of the kids. Do not punish them for their parent's shortcomings.

- Even if you have to grit your teeth to do it, honor the stepparent in your children's other home. Recognize that although you may not have desired that person to be part of your children's lives, he or she is. Be cordial and respectful in your encounters with the stepparent, as you would expect your children to be to any acquaintance. If your children's stepparent treats them kindly and with love, what more could you want? Children can never have too many people in their lives who love them.

- If you feel your children are being treated badly by their stepparent, take your concerns to your former spouse and the stepparent directly. Don't take potshots at the stepparent through the kids.

- Remember that fostering rebellion in your children against a parent or stepparent simply teaches them rebellion in other areas. As with anger and hatred, once children have learned to rebel in one situation or against one person, their rebellion will spread like wildfire and will come back to haunt the one who encouraged it.

Parents who abandon their relationships with their children in order to get out of dealing with their former spouse need to reevaluate. Divorce does not give you the right to disappear. Your children need you, and nothing will convince them that it is not their fault that you went away. Many custodial parents neglect the long-distance parent, cashing the child-support checks and sending the child to the long-distance parent every summer, but having little contact in between.

Solution Suggestions

- If either parent is long-distance and does not see the children very often, be creative in finding ways to make their long-distance relationship a strong one. Make sure your children feel loved by both parents as much as possible. If you are the custodial parent, help your children honor their other parent by re-membering to send gifts on birthdays and Father's Day or Mother's Day.

- Encourage your children to become pen pals with their stepsiblings and half-siblings and to call their stepparent and stepsiblings on their birthdays.

- Allow your children to talk freely with their other parent by phone as long as it is not during family mealtimes or after bedtime. Don't make an issue of the phone bill if it is long-distance. Six-hundred-minute phone cards are available for as little as twenty dollars.

- Allow children to email their other parent.

- Send noncustodial parents copies of the kids' best schoolwork, their report cards, and their artwork.

- Take pictures, and mail or email them. While I have to admit that I am not the world's best at this, it is important that I make an effort to keep my ex-husband up-to-date with what is happening in our children's lives.

- If you are a long-distance parent, find creative ways to keep your love visible during the times you are apart. My ex-husband, Mark, and his wife, Kathe, purchased a special silver charm bracelet for our twelve-year-old daughter, Jessica, that they plan to add engraved charms to as our beautiful girl grows.

- Mark makes sure that his summer times with Jessica and Joshua are special memories for them each year. Their family usually takes a summer vacation together, and Mark has developed activities with the kids like camping, Jet Skiing, and horseback riding that they don't usually get to do the rest of the year at our home.

Discussion Questions

1. In what ways have I worked to include my former spouse in our children's lives? Do I think of them as *my* children or *our* children?

2. If we have not been coparenting well, what things can I list now that I can start doing right away to better cooperate?

3. How do the children feel when we all attend functions and activities together? Are they able to enjoy us both, or are they tense and stressed? Do we make them feel bad when they want to sit with their other

parent or enjoy an activity alone with him or her? In what ways are we willing either to diffuse the tension or agree to attend some things separately?

4. How are we promoting a healthy relationship with our children's noncustodial parent? Are we maintaining contact regularly if they are long-distance through phone calls, mail, and email?

5. If everyone is local, are we as flexible as we can be with regard to our children's need and desire to spend time with both parents?

6. Whether my former spouse deserves it or not, what am I doing to improve my relationship with him or her? Am I letting my former spouse know about school activities and sports events? Am I inviting him or her to special occasions with our children? How can I better extend the olive branch of peace, even if every fiber of my being doesn't want to?

7. Am I asking the Lord regularly to show me where I can do a better job of coparenting? What has he been telling me?

8. Have I ever made the effort to include my children's other family in holiday get-togethers or birthday parties? Would it be possible to honor our children together in this way?

9. How am I making sure that I allow my children the freedom to talk openly about both households so that they do not feel forced to keep secrets from their other parent, which can teach them to be deceitful?

10. How am I going beyond conversation about scheduling to discuss with my former spouse any concerns about our children? Are we comparing notes on their physical, emotional, mental, and spiritual health?

12

Upholding Your Standards without Slamming Theirs

Don't quarrel with anyone. Be at peace with everyone,
just as much as possible.

—Romans 12:18 TLB

Scenario No. 1

Dad to son: Your mother said you couldn't see *Termi-nator 3* just because it's rated R? You're ten years old now, practically a man. Right, buddy? You're on my visiting time, so we don't have to listen to your mom when you're here. The next show is at two o'clock. Let's go.

Scenario No. 2

Mom to daughter: So, I can tell your father still hasn't quit that nasty smoking habit, has he? Your clothes reek. We'll have to wash everything in this suitcase. I suppose you didn't make it to church yesterday, either. Am I right?

The above scenarios are examples of parents who mean well, who probably think they are rightfully upholding their own standards, but who are actually insulting and undermining their child's other parent. They are causing their child to experience loyalty conflicts. Both scenarios are damaging to their child's emotional health and relationships with both parents, not just the parent doing the belittling.

In the first example, the father wants to please his son and show his son that his mother cannot control their time together. But while the son may be pleased at getting to go to the show, he now also has to carry guilt over disobeying his mother. He has to decide whether to bear the brunt of her anger if he admits that he went or deceive her by not telling her at all.

In the second scenario, the mother may have righteous anger that her daughter is exposed to secondhand smoke and that her spiritual training is neglected in her father's home. However, to express this in front of her daughter, and with the disdain that she obviously feels, creates defensiveness in her daughter toward her dad and anger toward her mom for being irritated about something over which the daughter has no control. Comments like these also begin to alienate the daughter from her father as she begins to be critical of his actions in order to try to please her mother.

Scenes like these are all too common and are a never-ending source of confusion and frustration for children of divorce, especially children being taught Judeo-Christian values in at least one of their parents' homes. How can children obey both parents, as they biblically are called to do, if parents issue opposite commands or if their actions do not match their words? If the children obey one, they are disobeying the other. If they love one, they often feel like they are betraying the other. They quickly begin to view their parents as hypocrites, smiling in church on Sunday, tearing each other apart throughout the week.

How could the parents in the above situations have handled things differently? In the first instance, the father could have told his son that he would need to see the movie first before he would know if it was appropriate for his ten-year-old. He could have called his son's mother, not because he needed her permission, but to get his son out of the hot seat of disobedience by informing her that he planned to take him to the show or to ask her to detail her objections. He could have compromised by taking his son to the theater, but to see a different show. Children

---

> How can children obey both parents, as they biblically are called to do, if parents issue opposite commands?

---

will always test your limits; however, they do not really expect them to bend. Children need firm boundaries to feel protected. You are not really the good guy, doing them or yourself any favor, by giving them what the other parent has denied.

In the second scenario, the mother should have focused on her pleasure at having her daughter home, not her dismay at the cigarette smell. She could have concentrated on the fun things her daughter got to do during her visit with her father, not the fact that they did not go to church. If the clothes needed to be washed, she did not need to make her daughter feel guilty or feel like a burden by stressing the fact. Instead, she could have tactfully put the clothes in the washing machine at a later time.

Last summer my ex-husband, Mark, and I experienced our first real parental conflict in years. Because he and

---

Children will always test your limits; however, they do not really expect them to bend. Children need firm boundaries to feel protected.

---

his wife work, I was concerned that twelve-year-old Jessica and eight-year-old Joshua would be spending a lot of time at his home unattended during their summer visit. I believed that the kids should be enrolled in a summer camp, daycare, or some other program where they would be supervised and would be doing something healthier than watching television and playing video games. When I brought up my concern, Mark bristled. I am sure that my tone was overbearing and insistent. He thought I wanted to run the show in his home, and he felt backed into a corner because most summer programs were already full or too expensive for his family to afford. He also thought that I was questioning his ability to make good decisions regarding the care of our children and that I thought I was doing a better job because I am able to stay home with them.

Before we knew it, we had slipped into old, bad habits we thought we had left behind years ago. We exchanged ugly words and insults and quickly digressed from the topic of summer to other parenting hurts and long-buried conflict. It was nasty, I am ashamed to say. Our only saving grace was that none of our children was around to hear us. I hung up on Mark after he threatened legal action, leaving him to believe the children would not even be visiting him.

After a quick prayer, the phone rang, and I started the conversation with my ex-husband again. I quickly tried to assure Mark that I did not want to control what went on in his home, that I only wanted the best for our children. This time, instead of thinking that I was accusing him of not giving our children the best, he heard my anxiety over the prospect of their being home alone for extended periods of time. He listened when I explained that Joshua was going through a difficult stage and that I was afraid Jessica would not be able to handle him.

We both apologized and encouraged each other that our primary goal was the same. Our methods may differ, but we both want the best for our children. Once we realized that we wanted the same thing, it was easy to come to agreement. I assured him that the children were certainly old enough to be left on their own some of the time, and Mark was careful to take them to work with him on many days rather than leave them alone too often. This turned out to be a great experience for Jessica, who got to help her dad with some aspects of his business.

Parents who are divorced from each other must remember that they cannot control what goes on in the other parent's home during their visitation. Bedtimes are likely to be different, and nutritional standards may vary. Your children may watch different television shows, go new places, hear different expressions and language, and meet people you would not choose for them to know. None of this is your business unless your children are exposed to illegal activity. One of the hardest things to accept with divorce is that you no longer have any right to say anything about what your former spouse does in his or her home, on his or her time with your children.

Being a divorced parent is a constant reminder that you are not in control. You never really were, but you can take comfort in the fact that you have an intimate relationship with the One who is. You can trust the God of this universe, who loves you and your precious children, to hold your children in the palm of his hand no matter where they are. You can plead for their protection, intercede for their safety, and ask him to instill in them wisdom and discernment. You can remember that they are really his children even more than they are yours, and you can trust him to look out for them.

You can work faithfully on improving your relationship with your former spouse so that you can come to agreement where the children are concerned. You can teach your children that doing right for right's sake is crucial, that loving the Lord is their highest calling. If your children have their own relationship with the Lord and you encourage them to maintain it through daily prayer, study of the Word, and devotions, he will guide them in difficult situations, whether those situations are found in their other parent's home, with peers, at school, or even with you. Give your children the assurance that their ultimate authority is God, and that they are called first and foremost to obey him. That way, if they are given conflicting orders from authority, they can know they are doing the right thing if they are doing what the Lord would have them do.

Common Problems to Consider

Parents who offer their children what is forbidden in the other parent's home encourage disobedience and deception.

Solution Suggestions

- Try to have a conversation with your former spouse about music you feel is acceptable for your children to listen to, television shows they can watch, movies they can see, and friends you think are good for them to spend time with. Ask for your spouse's opinions and be willing to listen with an open mind, rather than insisting upon what you think is right. You both still have the option of choosing your own standards in your own home, but at least you will know where the other parent stands.

- If you have any question at all about something happening in your child's life or an activity he or she wants permission to do, give the other parent the courtesy of a call to see what he or she thinks. It is better for your children not to have double standards.

- If your child does not want to see a movie or participate in an activity because he or she thinks the other parent would be angry, try not to push it. Either contact the parent and make the child comfortable, or change the activity.

- Instead of being angry that the other parent, even in his or her absence, seems to be controlling your life, be grateful instead that your child has such a sensitive conscience. It will stand them in good stead.

Give your children the assurance that their ultimate authority is God, and that they are called first and foremost to obey him.

Children who hear one parent criticize the other become defensive of that parent or alienated from a healthy relationship with that parent.

Solution Suggestions

- If one parent constantly tells the child how terrible the other parent is, the child will eventually develop a hardened heart. The child will be angry at the critical parent for knocking the other parent off the pedestal the child has placed the parent on and is likely to harden his heart against the parent being cut down. Speak positively or don't speak at all.

- Work to remember the characteristics you originally found attractive in your former spouse and praise those to your child. If your ex-husband is great at drawing and you can't draw a stick figure, praise that.

- Point out the good qualities in your child that remind you of your ex-spouse instead of harping on his or her flaws. If your child is great about picking up her dirty clothes and your former spouse was a neat freak, praise that good quality they have in common.

- Acknowledge that your love for your children's other parent was once real and vital, and that you still want to love your ex in a godly manner. Your children need to know that you loved each other, in order to know that they were created with love. Your children need to be able to trust in your love and the love of their other parent.

- Denigrating a child's parent makes the child wonder if he can trust the other parent's love. A child who cannot trust his parents has a very difficult time believing that he can trust God. Keep this in mind the next time an insult makes its way to the tip of your tongue.

Parents often forget that divorce means that each parent has the right to run his or her household in the way he or she sees fit, without interference from the former spouse. While you may not have the same moral standards, lifestyles, religious beliefs, ethics, or ways of doing things, you have to give up some control.

Solution Suggestions

- Remember that you can tell the other parent the way you do things at your home, but that doesn't mean he or she will do it that way at his or her house. The best way to ensure your children's well-being is to instill in them strong spiritual and moral values while they are with you. You can trust God to bring those values to fruition when your children face compromising situations in their parent's other home or anywhere outside your presence.

- Being a divorced parent is a great lesson in humility, a great reminder that you are not in control. Let go and let God. He can protect your children.

- Draw up a schedule of a typical week or day in your home and share it with your former spouse. Ask for one from him or her in return.

- Teach into situations your children encounter. If their other parent has a bad habit, encourage them to pray about it but not to judge because of it. All of us have bad habits. That's why we have need of a Savior.

- Ask the Lord to guard your tongue.
- If you have pointed out your former spouse's bad habits to your children or have spoken negatively and critically, apologize to your children and to your former spouse.
- Teach your children to be compassionate and loving, not critical. Your children should never be taught to look down on their other parent because they are not as "spiritual" as the people in your household. With the right attitude, your children can be a great witness to an unsaved parent. With a disdainful attitude, not only is their witness shot, but also conflict between families is more likely to occur.

Some parents play games with their children's schedule, purposely signing them up for activities that interfere with the other parent's visitation, accepting birthday party invitations on the other parent's time without consulting him or her first, and dangling special, fun outings in front of their children that can take place only if their children miss their scheduled visitation with their other parent. These tactics are cruel to the children and to their noncustodial parent.

Solution Suggestions

- Plan activities for your children only on your time. Period.
- If your child wants to join a sports team or try out for a play that would include practices, games, or performances on visitation days, make sure the other parent provides input *before* the child makes the decision to

join the team or audition for the play. Don't disappoint your child by allowing him or her to join, only to have to quit, making your former spouse the bad guy by having to tell your child no after he or she has already started.

- If you would like to switch a visitation period, be sure to ask, not inform, and give plenty of notice. Try to ask at least two weeks in advance. Do not demand the change, and be understanding if your former spouse already has plans for that time.

- Make sure that you are being reasonable when your former spouse needs to switch days.

- Plan your special occasions on your own time. If your family is planning a trip to Disney World, do not schedule it during the only two-week block your former spouse has with the children during the summer. There are fifty other weeks during the year that Disney World will be there for your family. Do not pull your children from their other parent.

- Do unto others—even your former spouse—as you would want them to do unto you.

Discussion Questions

1. How have I been guilty of trying to win my children away from their other parent? Do I need to apologize to my children or my former spouse?

2. Am I being fair in scheduling activities only on my own time and making sure I check with their other parent before the children schedule any activities on their other parent's time?

3. How am I observing the Golden Rule with my former spouse?

4. In what ways am I letting my children know that I once loved their other parent, that they were created with love, and that I am working on keeping a love for them as God would have me love them?

5. In what ways am I being too controlling of my former spouse?

6. Am I really trusting God with my children, even when they are away from me?

7. How have I tried to work with my former spouse to compare notes on standards for music, movies, friends, and dating? Have our conversations been constructive or destructive?

8. If we have not discussed our standards, am I willing to look for a window of opportunity?

9. Have I been encouraging my children to disobey their other parent when they are with me? What could I do to help us put the same boundaries in place for the kids in both households?

10. In what ways am I looking for the good things in my former spouse that I can praise to my children?

Part Four

THE AUTHORITIES

13

Praying through Panic

When Accusations Fly

> I cannot count the times when you have faithfully rescued me from danger. I will tell everyone how good you are, and of your constant, daily care.
>
> —Psalm 71:15 TLB

Scenario No. 1

Your heart beats funny. Your mouth goes very dry. Your hands feel damp and cold, and you breathe in short, shallow gasps. You see the car pull up in front of the house, watch the officers climb out, guns at their sides, notepad in hand,

and slowly approach your front door. You wonder what has happened now.

Scenario No. 2

You go to your children's school to pick them up at the end of the day, only to find they are not there. Their teacher says she is sorry. The principal looks confused. They knew it was your usual visitation day, but your former spouse told them there was a change of plans, and the kids seemed happy to see her, so they let them go. They did not think anything was amiss. You dial the number to your former spouse's home, but the line is disconnected. You race to her address, only to find an empty house.

Scenario No. 3

Your backbone is scraping against the slats of a hard, wooden chair. You raise your right hand and swear to tell the truth, the whole truth, and nothing but the truth as you sit on the witness stand facing your attorney. The judge peers over the spectacles perched on the end of his nose and shuffles disinterestedly through the pile of papers in front of him, the papers that contain all the gory details of the last few dysfunctional years of your marriage, divorce, and custody suit. Your eyes water, and you fight to keep composure as the judge considers severing your contact with your children.

Nothing about divorce is fun. Divorce with children is even more "not fun." Divorce with children when former spouses play dirty is the least fun of all. Yet it happens every day. Every day parents call their ex-husbands or ex-wives to

> Every day parents call their ex-husbands or ex-wives to arrange visitation with the children and get a disconnected number. Every day police officers show up at schools and homes to question children about their parents' behavior and interrogate parents about what happens in their home.

arrange visitation with the children and get a disconnected number. Every day parents out for revenge call authorities to investigate their former spouses for alleged abuse and neglect of their children. Every day police officers show up at schools and homes to question children about their parents' behavior and interrogate parents about what happens in their home. It is a nightmare for everyone who gets sucked into the middle of it, and it can destroy families individually and as a whole.

When any of the above situations occurs, a parent's natural instinct is to panic. Nothing is more gut-wrenching, soul-tearing, or heartbreaking than the idea of our children being harmed, kidnapped, or torn from our loving arms. With every divorce, however, these possibilities exist.

As Christians, we are called to love others, including our former spouses, before ourselves. As parents, we are to love and protect our children. In divorces in which both parties are able-minded and attempting to uphold a Christian standard, the worst should never occur. When one former spouse is out for revenge or has mental health issues, however, the worst can quickly become reality. Children become the hotly contended items in a divorce or post-divorce proceeding.

How do we know when to lay down our arms and when to pick them up and fight? When are we to turn the other cheek, and when do we stand our ground and demand accountability and justice?

When former spouses are difficult, argumentative, and even bitter, but visitation with our children is rolling along with as much anger as possible kept away from the children, we can turn the other cheek to insults and steer clear of the courtroom. But when our ability to parent our children is attacked unjustly, when allegations are false and might sever ties with our children, when children disappear and all communication is cut off, it is time to defend ourselves and take aim with the truth.

What weapons should a Christian use?

- *Prayer.* You and your spouse can pray for God's favor and for an ongoing or restored relationship with all of your children.

- *Intercessory prayer.* Friends, family members, and your church can intercede on your behalf, especially during court hearings.

- *Specific Scripture prayer.* You don't have to ask God for a specific outcome, but you can be specific in praying Scripture over the situation. For example, Adam and I frequently asked for "wisdom and discernment" for the psychologists and judges who had to determine which party was telling the truth. We asked the Lord to guard our tongues so that only truth issued from them. He was faithful every time.

- *Faith.* As Christians, we must have faith that God is good, that he loves us, and that he loves our children. If we do not trust his promises when things seem the worst, what is the point of even trying?

- *Scripture.* When Adam and I faced court hearings that could have severed all ties to his daughters, and it was our word against his former wife's, the Lord gave

The Lord, the courts, and the agencies are looking for the party with "clean hands," the one who is telling the truth.

us many Scriptures that seemed to have been written specifically for us. The book of Psalms, especially, was comforting, as we echoed David's cries for the Lord to deliver us from this adversarial position.

- *The truth.* The Lord, the courts, and the agencies are looking for the party with "clean hands," the one who is telling the truth. If you stand on the truth, even when twisting it a little would appear to benefit you legally, God will honor it.

- *Direct communication and reconciliation.* Directly communicating concerns and problems to your former spouse before they reach the stage of legal action saves everyone headaches and heartaches. Do everything in your power to live in peace.

- *Mediation.* If you and your former spouse cannot negotiate in good faith by yourselves but do not want to end up in court, mediation might be an option. Mediators take time with both parties and present "offers" back and forth, attempting to negotiate an agreeable settlement on issues you could not solve yourselves.

- *Fasting.* When we sacrifice food for a short period of time and substitute prayer for a particular situation, God can use the sacrifice in a powerful way.

- *Friends and family.* Lean on those who love you for their consolation, advice, and support.

- *Attorneys.* When a former spouse refuses visitation, violates court orders, or is a true danger to your children, seek the best legal counsel you can find and afford.

- *Counselors.* If you find a counselor who is well trained in stepfamilies, counseling can be very beneficial in helping you relieve negative emotions and strategize an effective game plan. A counselor can also testify on your behalf or submit a report to the court if necessary.

- *The court.* A Christian can feel comfortable bringing legal action against a former spouse if direct communication, mediation, and other attempts to rectify the situation have been exhausted and a relationship with your children is being damaged or denied.

- *The Internet.* The Internet has a wealth of resources on a variety of subjects such as custody issues, false allegations, kidnapped kids, mental health issues, postdivorce recovery, and attorneys.

- *Legal knowledge.* Parents facing legal challenges that could cost them their kids must get educated about the situation they face in order to help their attorney help them. What are the statutes in your state that cover family court? What is the standard guideline for visitation in your local court district? What judge will you have? How does your judge usually rule? What experience has your attorney had with your judge?

- *Investigators.* If your children have been taken away by a former spouse and you have a court-ordered right to visitation or custody, do not hesitate to try to find them.

- *Thick skin.* If your former spouse is bitter and you want to avoid courtrooms and attorneys, you may have to develop a thick skin and learn to calmly absorb insults

---

Children are not weapons to be used to get back at a
former spouse. Every negative word children hear about
their parent destroys a part of those children.

---

and accusations, as long as they are not interfering
with your relationship with your children. Ugly talk
is relatively normal; refusing visitation is not.

What weapons should Christians *not* use?

- *The children.* Children are not weapons to be used
  to get back at a former spouse. Every negative word
  children hear about their parent destroys a part of
  those children. Parental alienation syndrome is an
  actual tactic of some bitter, angry parents who speak
  so badly of their former spouse for so long that the
  children are "programmed" to believe every word and
  hate the other parent. Studies have shown this almost
  always destroys a child's self-esteem and potential for
  healthy long-term relationships as an adult.
- *Friends and family.* Putting friends and family members in the middle of arguments between you and your
  former spouse is just about as cruel as using the children.
  Allow friends and family members to be neutral parties
  if they need to be. Remember at all times, no matter
  what pressure you are under, the goal is to "speak the
  truth in love" (Eph. 4:15).
- *False allegations of physical or sexual abuse or neglect.*
  No child should ever, *ever* be put through the agony
  of being questioned by police officers regarding a parent's behavior, disciplinary methods, or ways of showing physical affection. The only time child protective

183

investigators should be called in is when a parent *is absolutely certain* that something dangerous is occurring in the other home and all other attempts to rectify the situation have been exhausted. In an investigation, children are questioned alone regardless of their age or how frightened they are, and they must sometimes take off their clothes. This is one of the cruelest things I have ever witnessed being done to a child, and it leaves a permanent impression of suspicion in the child's mind of the parent being accused. Using allegations as a weapon or a fishing expedition to try to make a former spouse look bad destroys your own children's innocence.

- *Police officers or any law enforcement agency.* As with false allegations of abuse to state child protective agencies, false reports to police of abuse, threats, stalking, and other alleged criminal behavior are destructive and usually counterproductive to the one making them. Put yourself in your little ones' shoes when an officer knocks on the front door, frowning, looking serious and scary, and questions them and their parent. If you file false reports just because you are angry or trying to get ahead in a court battle, I guarantee they will come back to haunt you.

- *The court.* While going to court may be necessary to defend yourself against false accusations, restore visitation with your children if it is being denied, or bring your children back to you if they have been taken away, it should never be used as a weapon against your former spouse. All court actions are lengthy, expensive, and emotionally costly. They make an already difficult relationship even more hostile, because someone will lose each hearing. First Corinthians 6 admonishes Christians for taking each other to court. Use the courtroom as an absolute last resort if your children or your relationship with your children is in danger.

- *Lies.* "You shall not give false testimony against your neighbor" (Exod. 20:16). This is one of the Ten Commandments. God hates lies. That should be enough for you to know to steer clear of this "weapon." It will backfire, and it shows not only a total disregard for the Word of God, but also a complete lack of trust in him to take care of the situation without your "help."

Common Problems to Consider

My former spouse is so hostile that she uses the children as weapons against me, withholding visitation to ask for more money or just refusing out of spite to turn over the kids.

Solution Suggestions

- If you owe child support, be faithful to pay it and pay it on time. No matter how much you hate to pay child support, if it is your legal obligation, release the money and ask God to bless your children with it. If your child support was awarded unfairly and you can prove it, go back to the judge. In the meantime, do not complain about it to your former spouse or your children. It will just make your children feel like a burden.
- If you do not receive your child support or think you need extra money, never withhold or threaten

to cut off visitation for lack of payment. Not only is this cruel to your children and their other parent, but it is also illegal and may cost you custody of your children. Rectify the monetary situation through legal means, but play fair with the children's visitation and keep your mouth shut about finances in front of them.

- Keep a short log of all phone calls to and from your former spouse and what was discussed regarding the kids and visitation. In extreme cases of unrelenting hostility in front of the children, you may feel it necessary to inform your former spouse that you will be recording phone calls. *Be very careful to learn the law and follow it if you take this extreme measure. Recording calls is a federal offense if the party is not informed before conversation begins that he or she is being recorded. In fact, in many states, you must go beyond informing and ask for consent. If your former spouse refuses to give consent, do not record.*

- Record every occasion when visitation is refused or the children are brought home late or picked up early. Diaries of these events are crucial to custody cases if you are unable to reach an amicable agreement and must go to court.

- If your children are being withheld from you because of money or for any other unjust reason, do everything you can personally to rectify the situation, and if all else fails, consider taking legal action. The courts provide remedies for parents who are denied time with their children, such as make-up visitation, an increase of visitation days, or even a change of custody.

My former spouse is so bitter toward me that she is constantly belittling me to my face, on the phone, and especially in front of the children. She has told so many lies about my behavior to my teenager that she is refusing to visit me at all. I have not had contact with my daughter in months.

Solution Suggestions

- Ask your former spouse for a face-to-face meeting in a neutral location. Take a close friend or family member with you to witness the conversation, and keep emotions in check. Ask your former spouse for assistance in enforcing the visitation, whether the teenager wants to come or not. Stay away from blame and accusations. Anything that has already been said or done does not matter. It is the future that needs to be worked out.

- If you are a father being denied visitation, never go to your former spouse's home for confrontation or allow her to enter yours. Go to neutral locations where there are plenty of people, and take someone with you. Our culture is so conditioned to believe that men are violent that you never want to be caught in a situation in which accusations could be made and it would be your word against hers.

- With gentle firmness, remind your former spouse that allowing the children to refuse to visit is not an option if visitation was awarded to you. It is the custodial parent's job to ensure that kids get to visitation on time, each time. The decision is not up to the child, and teens are still technically children. It is the parent's responsibility to obey the rules.

- Bring a tape recorder if you think the conversation needs to be remembered exactly. If you turn it on, make sure that your former spouse can see it and that you have informed him or her that you are recording. Otherwise, you may be breaking the law. If people know their words are being recorded, the hostility level is likely to drop considerably.

- Find a family counselor or therapist who specializes in parental alienation syndrome. Tell your former spouse that you will pay for sessions for you and your child in order to aim for reconciliation. If your former spouse refuses to allow the child to have counseling and you have to take legal action to see your child, it will not look good that the former spouse refused to allow the child to counsel with you.

- During the time that you have no visitation with your children, keep in touch in ways that are within your control. Drop cards in the mail and send presents for special occasions. Attempt to reach your children by phone. Pray without ceasing.

- If a child refuses to visit you and legally you are unable to restore the relationship, do not get discouraged or give up even if you know the mail is intercepted, the presents unopened, and the phone calls refused. Rejection is terrible, but God can restore.

- If you believe that mail to your child is intercepted by your former spouse, make copies of cards and letters before you send them and keep them in a file or shoe box. Your child will appreciate them one day.

- If all else fails, go to mediation or court. Pull out all the stops to have a relationship with your child. Even if the legal authorities allow the child to remain out of your life, you will be able to rest assured knowing you exhausted every avenue. Someday your child will also know you tried everything.

This afternoon a child protective worker and police officer showed up at my door and said they needed to talk to me about an alleged "incident" that happened in our home. They wanted to come in and interview me and the children. I didn't know what to do. I was scared, and that made the children terrified. They started to cry.

Solution Suggestions

- In cases like this, do not panic. If you are the step-parent, ask the authorities at the door to wait just a minute while you call your spouse and attorney. Take a minute to collect yourself and pray. The people at the door are not out to get you; they are just fact-finding and doing their jobs.
- Reassure your children. Their reactions to the knock on the door may range from mildly curious to hysterically afraid. Let them know that you will handle the situation and it will be fine. Ask them to go to their rooms or to a room where they cannot hear any conversation you have with the officers at the door.
- Know the laws in your state regarding searches and interrogation of children. Without your permission, the officers may not enter your home. However, if you refuse permission and the authorities have

probable cause to believe children are in danger, they have the right to remove the children from your home.

- Rather than opening the door and welcoming the officers in, step outside with them. Try to ascertain what accusations have been raised before you make a decision on allowing them to enter.

- Ask the officers to wait for your spouse to arrive. In child protective investigations, normally everyone in the family must be questioned. Officers usually do not mind waiting for both adults, because it saves them a second trip. Also, having your spouse with you helps you stand strong.

- If you have an attorney, call him and ask him to speak to the officers at your door. Allow him to glean information from them, and then follow his advice if you trust him. Usually attorneys will advise that if you do not have anything to hide, you should let them come in. However, do not blindly follow this advice, as many false allegations are believed and prosecuted.

- If you have spoken with the officers and they just need to be reassured that your children are fine, bring the children to the door or outside to them. Sometimes just laying eyes on the children to ascertain their well-being is enough.

- Know your rights ahead of time. If your relations with your former spouse are so contentious that anything is possible, arm yourself ahead of time. Research the laws in your state regarding abuse investigations, denied visitation, and alienation. Being naive gets you nowhere in a legal fight.

- If you allow the officers into your home to question you, be forthright without drowning them in details. Tell the whole truth.

- Bring out a tape recorder and ask to record the questioning. If you have it on tape, no one can testify that you said something you did not say. If you do not record the questioning, at least take notes.

- After the authorities leave, journal everything you can remember that transpired and was said.

- When the officers leave, ask them to show your children the lights on top of their car or to turn on their siren. Lighten the occasion for your children's sake, and do not communicate fear of authority to them.

- After the officers are gone, pull your children close and reassure them again that the misunderstanding will be cleared up soon. Allow children to ask questions and talk about what happened as much as they want to, but do not dwell on it. Do something fun.

- If a child has falsely accused you of physical abuse under his or her other parent's direction, the child will likely carry a lot of guilt or anger. Take that child aside and simply love him or her. If you are accused of sexual abuse, express physical affection only in front of other adults. Be as proactively protective as you can for yourself and your child. Let the accuser know you love him or her unconditionally, but also teach biblical lessons on the importance of telling the truth. If the child asks for forgiveness, grant it freely, and keep your anger toward your former spouse away from your child.

- Anger that mounts when children are used by former spouses as accusers against you can run white-hot. It literally sears your soul and can cause you to come as close to wanting to physically hurt someone as you ever will again in your life. Find a healthy outlet as quickly as you can to take the pressure off. Go outside and scream. Hit a punching bag. Go to the gym. Find a listening ear to vent into. Cry out to God and don't quit until he calms your spirit.

- Avoid contact with your former spouse until you have had time to process everything that has happened and calm down. *Do not* call your former spouse. Doing so will only fuel the fire, and he or she can then turn around and accuse you of threatening, harassing, or stalking. Calling will only make things worse for you.

Discussion Questions

1. How am I doing everything in my power to keep relations between my former spouse and myself as amicable as possible for the children's sake?
2. Am I fulfilling my child support obligation? Do I pick up and return the children on time? Am I respectful of their other parent? In what ways am I trying to avoid ever becoming so contentious that we have to go back to court?
3. Have I used the children to get back at my former spouse? Do I need to apologize and make amends to my children and my ex-spouse and allow them more time to be together?
4. Have I educated myself to be prepared if I am ever unjustly accused of wrongdoing? Do I know what

the laws are in my state regarding searches, visitation, and alienation?

5. How am I protecting myself from any possible allegations? Am I using a calm voice when speaking to my ex-spouse, avoiding all confrontations and any possibility of being accused of harassment or stalking?

6. How are we making sure that our family is not isolated, that others see us interacting and having a good time? If we are not participating in activities, do not attend church, and spend most of our time with only each other, there is no one who can come forward and vouch for us if necessary.

7. In what ways am I preparing myself for the possibility that authorities might come to my door and ask questions someday? Have I talked with my spouse about how we would handle it?

8. Do we know where we would draw the line, such as in refusing to allow officers to strip our children, even if drawing that line might mean we would be arrested or the children removed? Do we have relatives who would drop everything and come immediately to take the children if this occurred?

9. In what ways am I showing my child that I love her, even if she has cut off communication with me for the time being? Is my anger preventing me from being in constant prayer that we will be reconciled?

10. Am I reaching out in the ways that I can through mail, email, and phone calls? Have I considered counseling or taking legal action to restore this relationship?

14

Taking God to Court

Telling the Truth and Minimizing the Damage

> What a tangled web we weave when we seek to interpret legally "Do unto others."
>
> —Paul Harvey

In January 1996 Adam began having difficulty visiting with my three stepdaughters. He would try to arrange to see them, but he and his ex-wife could not come to an agreement. Because no set visitation was established, Adam hired an attorney to try to establish one. In February of that year, authorities entered our lives when an allegation of abuse was filed against Adam. In March 1996, at the first post-divorce court hearing, the allegations of abuse were dismissed and a visitation schedule was established.

For the next three years, we had court hearings on everything from back child support to more abuse allegations. The visitation request became a full-blown custody battle. Before it was over, guardian ad litems were appointed for the three girls, and for three years we had guardians and agencies quizzing, questioning, and observing all seven of our family members and the adults and children in Adam's former wife's home. All four adults and the three girls underwent psychological evaluations and testing, and we had family sessions with a court-appointed psychologist. We trooped in and out of the Clearwater, Florida, courthouse more times than I care to remember. It makes my stomach clench to this day to have to enter a courthouse for any reason.

Adam and I married, had baby Justin, and nursed my mother until her death with cancer throughout this same period. I was also in the middle of finishing my master's degree, and we were both trying to support our family of eight. It was the most stressful time in my life, more stressful in many ways than my own divorce. In January 1999, primary residence of the three girls changed to my husband.

While I would never recommend fighting legally except as a last resort, for many reasons, we were reassured along the way that it was important to see the battle through to the bitter end. If you choose this method, keep in mind that *bitter* is the key word in these court fights. Long after the judge issues a final ruling, the bitterness lives on in emotionally battered ex-spouses, yourself, and the children who got caught in the crossfire.

Would we do it all over again? I don't know. But if we had to do it again, we would make a stronger effort to reconcile

---

Long after the judge issues a final ruling, the bitterness lives on in emotionally battered ex-spouses, yourself, and the children who got caught in the crossfire.

---

outside of the courtroom. We would get better educated up front to avoid costly legal mistakes that occurred and dragged out the proceedings and potential for damage. We would take more precautions to protect ourselves and our children. We would know what to do with the anger and heartbreak rather than unleash them on our former spouses, our children, or each other. We would be on our knees constantly instead of having to be brought to them by the events.

For anyone considering post-divorce proceedings regarding your children, be forewarned that these actions take a long time and do a lot of damage, especially when former spouses play out the drama through the children, keeping them informed of every legal shot fired and destroying children's trust. If your children are in physical danger, if they are being neglected, if their academic standing is suffering due to excessive absences, or if the custodial parent has untreated mental health issues or is cutting off visitation with the children, you may decide litigation is your only choice in order to protect your children. However, use it only after much prayer and only as a last resort.

If you need to proceed legally to retrieve your children, find your children, or protect your children, get educated before you start. Adam initially made the mistake of hiring an attorney after a free consultation simply because the man's firm advertised that they helped dads with custody issues. Unfortunately, it was only after Adam had signed the contract, spent thousands of dollars, and lost more ground with his children than he gained that he found out this attorney had no custody trial experience and had dropped every one of his clients as soon as he had run through the amount of money they said they could afford to spend, regardless of how far along their case was. (We eventually sued the attorney and did not have to pay his bill.)

Ask family members and friends for recommendations of attorneys. Find out who in your church practices family law. Ask for free initial consultations, and visit several law firms. Compare hourly rates and estimates of how much your case will cost. Ask them how many custody trials they have won for their clients. Ask what experience they have had with your judge and their impressions of him or her (you do not want to hire an attorney your judge cannot stand). Find an attorney that specializes in your special circumstances. If you are faced with allegations of abuse, has your attorney successfully defended others who have been charged with

---

If you need to proceed legally to retrieve your children, find your children, or protect your children, get educated before you start.

---

similar allegations? If you are a dad trying to obtain custody, does your law firm specialize in helping dads?

Go to your local courthouse's law library, buy family law books at a local law school, study books borrowed from your local library, or get information online. Each state's statutes are available online. If you want to be intimately involved with your case, make sure you hire an attorney who will allow that. Many attorneys file motions first and tell their clients later. Our preference was to see each item our attorney planned to send before he sent it. That way we could correct dates and details before they became an incorrect part of the court record.

We also did a lot of the legwork in our own case for our attorney by drafting letters, keeping journals, and offering suggestions. Many attorneys will not allow you to be this

---

Make sure that you and your attorney will be comfortable with the level of hands-on involvement you choose. These are your children, and this is your case. You do not want an attorney who makes arbitrary decisions with which you might not agree.

---

involved, but our case was intricate enough that we felt it crucial to be very involved. Make sure that you and your attorney will be comfortable with the level of hands-on involvement you choose. These are your children, and this is your case. You do not want an attorney who makes arbitrary decisions with which you might not agree.

Also, as a Christian, you should question your attorney as to his or her values and stance on Christianity. High-powered attorneys with weak ethical standards may win your case for you, but they may win it by bulldozing everyone in their way, from your former spouse to your children. Make sure your attorney's strategy is one that would win approval from the Lord as well as win in the courtroom. Let your attorney know up front that you plan to fight a good fight, with no dirty tactics such as mudslinging and false allegations. Stand on the truth, and aim to be the party with the "clean hands."

Finally, if you do end up in a lengthy court battle, make sure that you take time for your marriage and for the uninvolved children in the home. It is easy to get swept up in the chaos of custody battles, the agony of allegations, and the misery of missing children and forget that you still have others who need you, now more than ever. Call in reinforcements, such as grandparents and close friends, when you need a break or to get your uninvolved children out of the line of fire, but keep a balance. What is happening in your family is affecting them too. Love them, keep them informed in ways that are age-appropriate, pray with them, and find ways to have fun with them.

Common Problems to Consider

My ex-husband has not visited our children in years. My new husband would like to adopt them.

Solution Suggestions

- If your children are young, and you do not anticipate your former spouse ever wanting to be an active part of their lives, pray about it and consider it.
- If you know your former spouse's whereabouts, give him the courtesy of a letter or personal phone call before taking any action. See how he feels about it.
- Know that terminating parental rights to allow for adoption also terminates a parent's child support obligation to you.
- Make sure your new husband is fully aware of the responsibility he is taking on, that he would be the children's parent if something were to happen to you.
- If the children are old enough, ask their opinion. Let them know that their dad loves them but is unable or unwilling to be in their lives and that their stepparent would like to step into that role for them. Tell them

it would mean changing their last name, and see how they feel. Allow them to ask questions.

- Do not ask your children's opinion if you are not prepared to honor their feelings. If they say no, and you and your husband proceed anyway, you may create hard feelings.

I just received a petition in the mail that my former spouse now wants custody of our children. I don't know what to do. I can't afford to fight, and I do not want to lose my children.

Solution Suggestions

- Get on your knees. Ask God how he wants you to proceed. You normally have at least fifteen to twenty days to respond to any petition. Use the time wisely to gear up for battle or to face gracefully giving in.
- If you must fight, start investigating and start saving. See if you can get a loan from a family member or a bank, if necessary. Ask friends, family, and your church for the right attorney for you. Check out your state's laws and preferred visitation schedules.
- Examine your own heart and the problems in your home. Examine the problems you have with your former spouse. Ask for discernment in figuring out the motive for this suit. Are there ways you need to be parenting better? Have you been denying visitation without legal right to do so? Is your former spouse justified or out for revenge?
- Try to stop the fight before it enters the courtroom. If you know that what your ex wants is really more coparenting with you or an extra visitation day a week,

find ways to compromise before allowing a judge to decide for you.

I have been falsely accused of abusing my children, and I am being taken to court to have all visitation revoked. I am petrified that I am going to lose my kids.

Solution Suggestions

- One Christian counselor told us in a session recently, "Don't be afraid to trust in what you know." God is a good God. He is a just God. He is faithful. He wants justice for your children as much as you do. Hearings may not go the way you expect. Visitation may be cut off for periods of time. Still, God is God. And God is good. Lean on him with every ounce of your being. Wait for his answer.

- Protect yourself. If you are being accused of being an angry parent, make sure a lot of people see your family interacting and having fun. If you are being accused of being an alcoholic, don't drink that single glass of wine with dinner anymore. Romans 12:17 says to be careful to do what is right in the eyes of everybody. That way no one will have any accusation that can stand.

- Get a video camera and take a lot of pictures. If your family is a normal, loving family, document it. Then if kids are pressured by one parent to tell authorities or guardian ad litems how miserable they are in your home, you can prove differently. If you never have to use the tapes and pictures in a legal fight, you can relive your children's childhoods for years to come and will have something to show your grandchildren someday.

- Ask to tape record or video record all questioning by authorities and agencies.
- Do not be fake. When guardians come to observe your family, act as normal as possible.
- Give truthful answers, but do not expand your answers too much. Do not give so much detail that decision makers can't keep your story straight.
- Know your legal remedies. If you lose a hearing, are you prepared to appeal? Do you know what your rights are?

My former spouse has disappeared with my children. Their phone is disconnected; their house is empty. I am scared, angry, and shocked.

Solution Suggestions

- Make sure you are okay. Get with your spouse and call trusted friends and family over for prayer. Get with God and give your children back to him. Remind yourself that they are his children, and he knows exactly where they are. This is one of those times when God is saying, "How much do you really trust me?" Trust him with all your might, and lean not on your own understanding. In all your ways acknowledge him, and he will direct your paths (Prov. 3:5–6).
- Gather together all the information you can find. If you have license numbers for your former spouse's vehicles, give them to authorities. If you have social

security numbers, photographs, and contact information for relatives of your ex, report them as well.

- Call your children's grandparents, aunts, uncles, or any friends of your former spouse you can find. Ask if they know their whereabouts.
- Send recent pictures of your children to the national center for missing children. The National Center for Missing and Exploited Kids can be found at www.missingkids.com.
- Check with your children's school to see if they are still attending or have been withdrawn.
- Check with teachers and leaders of any extracurricular activities your kids participate in.
- Go to court and ask that custody change to you because your former spouse has fled. If you win custody, also ask for a pick-up order that allows law enforcement agencies to pick up your children from the former spouse wherever they are found.
- Wait on the Lord, and pray for your children's protection. Ask him to help you deal with your anger and helplessness so that when your children are found, you can be fairer to their other parent than that parent was to you. Revenge, when children are involved, is never sweet.

Discussion Questions

1. Do I have up-to-date information that would help me find my children if they were ever missing? Do I know my former spouse's address, phone numbers, and workplace; our children's school, teacher, and

medical providers; and extended relatives' phone numbers and addresses? Do I know my former spouse's license plate number, birth date, and social security number and have them readily available?

2. Do I have up-to-date pictures of all of my children along with their fingerprints?

3. How much do I really trust the Lord to fight on my children's behalf? Am I angry with him or am I able to lean on him? In what ways can I draw closer and allow him to handle my emotions and reactions?

4. In what ways am I trying to find an attorney who fits my case, my faith, my finances, and my standards? Am I willing to do the legwork involved before jumping in and signing the first contract put in front of me?

5. How am I making sure that my attorney is not crossing ethical lines that I would not cross?

6. Do I have an attorney who has a good track record for cases like mine? Is he familiar with the judge? Has he had run-ins with my judge? Is he open to allowing me to prepare some of my own case with him?

7. How am I financially strategizing so that a court case or investigation of missing children will not also cost me my home and my livelihood?

8. Am I keeping a journal of events during the time of any investigation or period when my children are missing?

9. How am I keeping things as normal as possible for the other children in my home when we are under fire? Am I relieving their anxiety, praying with them, and having fun with them even if I don't feel like it?

10. In what ways am I protecting my marriage now that my former spouse has once again thrust chaos into our midst?

15

Preserving Children Caught in the Crossfire

Step In, Step Back, or Step Down?

> I have fought the good fight, I have finished the race,
> I have kept the faith.
>
> —2 Timothy 4:7

Trying to keep your family intact and your children emotionally stable while going forward with any kind of litigation that involves some of your children is a delicate balancing act. It requires constant reevaluation along the way, ensuring that you are walking the straight and narrow with God in front leading the way, your spouse by your side, and your children underneath the umbrella of protection as much as possible. If you are in a situation in which you sense that relations with your former spouse are getting worse instead of better, or your children are losing ground at a dangerous pace, you will have to decide: Is it time to step in, step back, or step down?

Stepping In

Stepping in as an attempt to change the balance of power between you and your former spouse regarding the care and keeping of your children is never easy. You must be prepared for the high price it will exact in terms of your time, energy, finances, and emotions. You and

---

Make sure that you have worn calluses on your knees first, asking God for guidance before you decide to take action.

---

your new spouse need to be in agreement before action is taken, or trying to save your children could cost you your marriage. Make sure that you have worn calluses on your knees first, asking God for guidance before you decide to take action.

If you plan to try to increase your visitation time or change custody through the court system, the following criteria should be met first:

- You sense peace after prayer about your decision.
- You have exhausted all other options first (direct communication and negotiation with your former spouse, mediation, etc.).

- Your spouse agrees to support the action you are taking.

- You know that a lengthy court action will not cripple you financially.

- You know the laws of your state and the likelihood for success or failure.

- You have an attorney who you absolutely trust, who knows the laws, knows your case, and has worked with you toward a solution.

- You firmly believe that your children are in a dangerous situation without this change: Their academic progress is suffering greatly, they have become extremely rebellious, visitation has ended, or some other extreme circumstance exists. (Just wanting more time with your kids is not usually legal ground to obtain it, especially if the divorce has already been finalized and a visitation schedule set. The best way to get extra time is to work with your former spouse to obtain it.) Or your former spouse has untreated mental health issues that are negatively affecting your children in ways you can document. Or your former spouse or his or her new partner is physically or sexually abusive. Or your former spouse is neglecting the children. Or your former spouse is involved in illegal activities.

- You realize that your children will be damaged by a fight but believe that they are being more damaged by not fighting. Courts must have evidence that children are in serious trouble before making changes, especially a change of custody. That means your children must visibly deteriorate before there is ground for the court to make a change. This is one of the toughest things to watch. One child we know, for example, had more than forty absences in one school year (and was not sick), and her mother had not allowed the teen to visit her father in years despite court-ordered visitation. Yet those circumstances were not considered serious enough for the court to change custody.

- You are willing to gather information and evidence without making your children uncomfortable, crossing legal lines, or harassing your former spouse. You are up to the task of journaling, logging phone calls, and keeping track of medical appointments and academic progress and attendance.

Stepping Back

If you have been pursuing your former spouse legally or just hounding him or her for more than you were ordered to have, and your children are not in dire straits, it may be time to consider stepping back. Stepping back can provide a time of reevaluation, prayer, and regrouping. If the fighting is about to end your marriage, stepping back can help you preserve your marriage before returning to the battle. Stepping back may be the best thing to do if you know your children's situation is not the best, but the fight is harming them or causing them to hate you.

If you have been considering a legal fight or are in the middle of one already, it may be time to step back if the following events are occurring:

- Your children's situation with your former spouse is improving. While it may make a better legal case for you if your children suffer in ways that can be documented while in the care of your former spouse, it is always better for the children for their parents to improve.

- You realize that your motives have been to "get" your former spouse, not to look out for your children's best interests.
- You no longer have peace about the fight.
- You sense a window of opportunity for negotiations outside of the courtroom. It is always better for couples to decide themselves how they are going to parent rather than giving the courts the decision-making power.
- You see that the damage to your relationship with your former spouse is so great that your children are being put through the wringer.

Stepping Down

The hardest decision you may have to make is whether to step down from fighting for your children altogether. If fighting to the bitter end is going to be more negative than positive for all involved, throw in the towel. Once you have searched for missing children for as long as time, emotions, and finances will allow, give them to God and let go. If you have attempted to salvage the remnants of your children from the minefields that followed your divorce and have only succeeded at shredding the pieces that remain, give up your attempts to change the situation. Face your limitations and assess the cost for all involved of fighting anymore.

It may be time to step down if you find yourself in one or more of the following situations:

- Your children who were removed by a former spouse have not been located after valiant search efforts, and your financial and emotional reserves are dangerously low.

- You are losing the people you still have in your life (your spouse, remaining children or stepchildren, family, and friends) because of your efforts to regain the ones you do not have.

- The court is obviously ruling repeatedly against you, and your attorney advises that you really do not have a case.

- Your children have been alienated from you and think they hate you to the degree that forcing them to be with you might do more harm to all of you than good.

- You have been a long-distance or largely absent parent for some time, and your children have the chance to be adopted by a stepparent. While this may be a heart-wrenching decision to make, it may be in the best interests of your children.

- Fighting for your children has entrenched roots of bitterness in your heart so deeply that you are losing your relationship with the Lord and your perspective on what is right.

An Open Letter to Parents and Stepparents Caught in Ugly Legal Battles

Dear Moms, Dads, Stepmoms, and Stepdads,
I know you feel like your children are trapped in
a burning building and you have no way to get them

out. The authorities will not let you near them even though you would gladly sacrifice your life for theirs. You are weary of fighting, drained from the heavy financial burden and even heavier emotional toll that abuse allegations, custody litigation, or missing children is taking from your lives.

Sometimes, even though you feel guilty, you just want all your troubles to go away. You want peace restored in your home, in your marriage, and in your soul. Your pain is so great that you literally feel like your heart is breaking. Your anger is stronger and hotter than anything you have ever felt before. You feel betrayed by your former spouse, your children, and your God.

God is still there, and he is big enough to handle your rage and your pain. Pour yourself into him and beg for relief until you get some. Take action only where he leads and when he leads; give it everything you have.

In your new marriage, lean on each other. Discuss your rage and pain. Stepparents, talk about how robbed you feel of the joy that came with this new marriage. Express your disappointment and frustration at the interruption of your lives. Air your guilt in possibly not loving your stepchildren enough to want them if it takes this kind of heartache. Understand that your spouse loves these children more than the air he needs to breathe and be willing to help him fight the good fight so that he will not feel guilty later for not trying.

Walk together in the battle, and lean on the Lord and each other for strength. Do not allow the enemy another victory by tearing your marriage apart. You love each other, and you can be a shining example of what a redeemed family can be. The trials will not last forever. Resolution will come, even if it is not the outcome you hoped for or planned.

Be gentle and kind. Strive to take only one day—sometimes one hour—at a time, and surround yourselves with those who love you. Beg those around you to blanket you in prayer. Keep up your physical strength by eating well and regularly, and keep physically active. Rest as often as you can.

Be vigilant in your parenting, but also rest assured that God is watching over them every step of the way. Trust him.

In Christ,
A stepparent who has been there

Part Five

THE SUPPORT

16

Scriptures for Your Stepfamily

These commandments that I give you today are to be upon your hearts. Impress them on your children. Talk about them when you sit at home and when you walk along the road, when you lie down and when you get up.

—Deuteronomy 6:6–7

Nothing serves our families better than standing on Scripture in every situation. Here are some Scriptures organized by topics you might face. Quote them to yourself, your spouse, and your children. Memorize them together. Hang them around your home. They are the best protection you will find.

Love

> Hatred stirs up dissension,
> but love covers over all wrongs.

Proverbs 10:12

For God so loved the world, that he gave his one and only Son, that whoever believes in him shall not perish but have eternal life.

John 3:16

A new command I give you: Love one another. As I have loved you, so must you love one another.

John 13:34

Be devoted to one another in brotherly love. Honor one another above yourselves.

Romans 12:10

Love your neighbor as yourself.

Romans 13:9

Love is patient. Love is kind. It does not envy, it does not boast, it is not proud. It is not rude, it is not self-seeking, it is not easily angered, it keeps no record of wrongs. Love does not delight in evil but rejoices with the truth. It always protects, always trusts, always hopes, always perseveres. Love never fails.

1 Corinthians 13:4–8

And now these three remain: faith, hope and love. But the greatest of these is love.

1 Corinthians 13:13

Serve one another in love.

Galatians 5:13

But the fruit of the Spirit is love, joy, peace, patience, kindness, goodness, faithfulness, gentleness and self-control.

Galatians 5:22–23

Live a life of love, just as Christ loved us.

Ephesians 5:2

Love one another deeply, from the heart.

1 Peter 1:22

Whoever loves his brother lives in the light.

1 John 2:10

Dear friends, let us love one another, for love comes from God.

1 John 4:7

God is love.

1 John 4:8

If we love one another, God lives in us, and his love is made complete in us.

1 John 4:12

There is no fear in love. But perfect love drives out fear.

1 John 4:18

Peace

> I will lie down and sleep in peace,
>   for you alone, O LORD,
>   make me dwell in safety.

Psalm 4:8

> Consider the blameless, observe the upright;
>   there is a future for the man of peace.

Psalm 37:37

> I will listen to what God the LORD will say;
>   he promises peace to his people, his saints—
>   but let them not return to folly.

Psalm 85:8

> The fruit of righteousness will be peace;
>   the effect of righteousness will be quietness
>   and confidence forever.

Isaiah 32:17

Peace I leave with you; my peace I give you. I do not give to you as the world gives. Do not let your hearts be troubled and do not be afraid.

John 14:27

Let the peace of Christ rule in your hearts, since as members of one body you were called to peace. And be thankful.

Colossians 3:15

Now may the Lord of peace himself give you peace at all times and in every way. The Lord be with all of you.

2 Thessalonians 3:16

Protection from Enemies

[The LORD] defends the cause of the fatherless and the widow, and loves the alien, giving him food and clothing. And you are to love those who are aliens.

Deuteronomy 10:18–19

For the LORD watches over the way of the
righteous,
but the way of the wicked will perish.

Psalm 1:6

I lie down and sleep;
I wake again, because the LORD sustains me.
I will not fear tens of thousands
drawn up against me on every side.

Psalm 3:5–6

You are not a God who takes pleasure in evil;
with you the wicked cannot dwell.
The arrogant cannot stand in your presence;
you hate all who do wrong.
You destroy those who tell lies.

Psalm 5:4–6

But let all who take refuge in you be glad;
let them ever sing for joy.
Spread your protection over them,

that those who love your name may rejoice in
you.

Psalm 5:11

O LORD my God, I take refuge in you;
save and deliver me from all who pursue me.

Psalm 7:1

Note: The Psalms are filled with passages where David
cried out for God's mercy and protection. Study them in-
tensely. Refer to them often.

Patience

Wait for the LORD;
be strong and take heart
and wait for the LORD.

Psalm 27:14

A patient man has great understanding,
but a quick-tempered man displays folly.

Proverbs 14:29

The LORD is good to those whose hope is in him,
to the one who seeks him;
it is good to wait quietly
for the salvation of the LORD.

Lamentations 3:25–26

Let us not become weary in doing good, for at the proper time we will reap a harvest if we do not give up.

Galatians 6:9

We do not want you to become lazy, but to imitate those who through faith and patience inherit what has been promised.

Hebrews 6:12

Let us hold unswervingly to the hope we profess, for he who promised is faithful.

Hebrews 10:23

Kindness

> A kindhearted woman gains respect,
>   but a ruthless man gains only wealth.
> A kind man benefits himself,
>   but a cruel man brings trouble on himself.

Proverbs 11:16–17

> An anxious heart weighs a man down,
>   but a kind word cheers him up.

Proverbs 12:25

> If your enemy is hungry, give him food to eat;
>   if he is thirsty, give him water to drink.

Proverbs 25:21

If one falls down,
    his friend can help him up.
But pity the man who falls
    and has no one to help him up!

Ecclesiastes 4:10

"With everlasting kindness
    I will have compassion on you,"
says the Lord your Redeemer.

Isaiah 54:8

Return to the Lord your God,
    for he is gracious and compassionate,
slow to anger and abounding in love,
    and he relents from sending calamity.

Joel 2:13

He has showed you, O man, what is good.
    And what does the Lord require of you?
To act justly and to love mercy
    and to walk humbly with your God.

Micah 6:8

This is what the Lord Almighty says: "Administer true justice; show mercy and compassion to one another. Do not oppress the widow or the fatherless, the alien or the poor. In your hearts do not think evil of each other."

Zechariah 7:9–10

Be kind and compassionate to one another, forgiving each other, just as in Christ God forgave you.

Ephesians 4:32

Make sure that nobody pays back wrong for wrong, but always try to be kind to each other and to everyone else.

1 Thessalonians 5:15

Hard Work/Working Together

You are to help your brothers until the LORD gives them rest, as he has done for you.

Joshua 1:14–15

Just as each of us has one body with many members, and these members do not all have the same function, so in Christ, we who are many form one body, and each member belongs to all the others. We have different gifts, according to the grace given us. If a man's gift is . . . serving, let him serve; if it is teaching, let him teach; if it is encouraging, let him encourage; if it is contributing to the needs of others, let him give generously; if it is leadership, let him govern diligently; if it is showing mercy, let him do it cheerfully.

Romans 12:4–8

Share with God's people who are in need. Practice hospitality.

Romans 12:13

This service that you perform is not only supplying the needs of God's people but is also overflowing in many expressions of thanks to God. Because of the service by which you have proved yourselves, men will praise God for the obedience that accompanies your confession of the gospel of Christ, and for your generosity in sharing with them and with everyone else.

2 Corinthians 9:12

Serve one another in love. The entire law is summed up in a single command: "Love your neighbor as yourself."

Galatians 5:13–14

Carry each others' burdens, and in this way you will fulfill the law of Christ.

Galatians 6:2

We are God's workmanship, created in Christ Jesus to do good works, which God prepared in advance for us to do.

Ephesians 2:10

Obey [your earthly masters] not only to win their favor when their eye is on you, but like slaves of Christ, doing the will of God from your heart. Serve wholeheartedly, as if you were serving the Lord, not men, because you know that the Lord will reward everyone for whatever good he does.

Ephesians 6:6–8

Your attitude should be the same as that of Christ
Jesus:
Who, being in the very nature God . . .
made himself nothing,
taking the very nature of a servant.

Philippians 2:5, 7

Do everything without complaining or arguing, so that you may become blameless and pure, children of God without fault in a crooked and depraved generation, in which you shine like stars in the universe, as you hold out the word of life.

Philippians 2:14–16

Whatever you do, work at it with all your heart, as working for the Lord, not for men.

Colossians 3:23

Anger/Strife

In your anger, do not sin.

Psalm 4:4

Refrain from anger and turn from wrath;
do not fret—it leads only to evil.

Psalm 37:8

A quick-tempered man does foolish things.

Proverbs 14:17

A gentle answer turns away wrath,
but a harsh word stirs up anger.

Proverbs 15:1

A hot-tempered man stirs up dissension,
but a patient man calms a quarrel.

Proverbs 15:18

A hot-tempered man must pay the penalty.

Proverbs 19:19

Do not make friends with a hot-tempered man,
do not associate with one easily angered.

Proverbs 22:24

Do not be quickly provoked in your spirit,
for anger resides in the lap of fools.

Ecclesiastes 7:9

Do not take revenge, my friends, but leave room for God's wrath, for it is written: "It is mine to avenge; I will repay," says the Lord. On the contrary:

"If your enemy is hungry, feed him;
    if he is thirsty, give him something to
drink.
In doing this, you will heap burning coals on
his head."
Do not be overcome by evil, but overcome evil
with good.

Romans 12:19–21

Get rid of all bitterness, rage and anger, brawling and slander, along with every form of malice. Be kind and compassionate to one another, forgiving each other, just as in Christ God forgave you.

Ephesians 4:31–32

The Lord's servant must not quarrel; instead, he must be kind to everyone.

2 Timothy 2:24

My dear brothers, take note of this: Everyone should be quick to listen, slow to speak and slow to become angry, for man's anger does not bring about the righteous life that God desires.

James 1:19–20

17

Building Support

How to Network with Other Stepfamilies and Find Good Resources

> If he shall not lose his reward who gives a cup of cold water to his thirsty neighbors, what will not be the reward of those who by putting good books into the hands of their neighbors open to them the fountain of eternal life?
>
> —Thomas à Kempis

One of the biggest obstacles for stepfamilies in the church is that we feel like there is no one else like us. There are classes for singles, young adults, teens, children, and married couples. We even have divorce recovery classes. Yet it is still fairly rare to find a class for stepfamilies.

Stepfamilies need fellowship and support because the odds are so overwhelmingly against us. We need to find each other and bond so that we can shore up each other in times of trouble. Stepfamilies can find creative ways to network and work together. Here are some suggestions:

- If your church does not offer a stepfamily class, ask for one. If no one steps up to lead it, ask God if you should. Try to have your class meet during Sunday school hour or during Wednesday night services for maximum attendance.
- Go online or call churches in your area and ask if they have a stepfamily class or any resources for stepfamilies. When you find one that does, visit it. Talk to the leaders. Find out from participants what their experience has been. Visit www.successfulstepfamilies.com and download the article "Starting Your Local Ministry."
- Use the church bulletin to invite all stepfamilies to a stepfamily picnic at a local park. Ask everyone to bring a food item and drinks. You provide the paper goods and ice. Bring outdoor toys and games for the kids and have fun getting to know one another.
- Start a stepfamily web page where stepfamilies can post announcements and questions and get to know one another.
- Ask your church to pass around a sign-up sheet for those who want to be on a stepfamily list. Use the list to start a class, a Bible study, a prayer group, or a babysitting co-op.
- Help your church coordinate a special seminar for stepfamilies and bring in national speakers like Ron

---

Stepfamilies need fellowship and support because the
odds are so overwhelmingly against us.

Deal or myself, or sponsor a kids' workshop by Gary
Sprague or Linda Jacobs. Use Christian radio to invite
those beyond your four walls.

- If you hold a stepfamily seminar, be sure to collect
contact information and follow up with those who
attended. Your network of support might begin
there.

- Call national radio shows such as *Focus on the Family*
and *FamilyLife Today* and let them know you would
like to hear more programs geared toward stepfamilies. *Focus on the Family* can be reached at 800-A-
FAMILY (800-232-6459). *FamilyLife* can be reached
at 800-FL-TODAY (800-358-6329).

- To be really proactive, follow state and national legislation that pertains to families and marriage and let
politicians know which legislation you support and
which you want to see defeated.

For Dads Only

I salute Christian dads who are working hard to remain
an active part of their children's lives, either as custodial
dads or visiting parents. Never give up, and enjoy every moment with your children that you can. If your visitation is
ever taken away from you and your rights to your children
terminated, do not let that destroy you. Although you must
not violate court orders or restraining orders against you,
your love for your children can remain strong, even during

your separation from them. You can also pray that God will reconcile you somewhere along the way.

In the meantime, write letters to your children and keep them. They may want to read of your love for them someday. If you are not very good at writing, buy a mini-cassette recorder and talk into it. Tell your children all the things you would teach them if they were with you. Tell them stories of your parents and childhood. Keep the tapes in a safe place, and when God opens the door, you can present them.

Create photo albums or scrapbooks of your life so that your children can catch up one day on what you were doing while separated from them.

Here are a few resources just for you:

Dads Now

http://www.dadsnow.org

Dads Now is a proactive organization whose goal is to "grant to fathers the same right to be in the family as we have granted to women in the workplace." This site has lots of links to legal helps.

Fatherville

http://www.fatherville.com

Fatherville is about everything "dad," from parenting tips to chat groups.

The Father Resource Network

http://www.father.com

This site provides a network of referral and resource support services to help solve the problems and challenges associated with fatherhood today.

Resources for Stepfamilies

Films

Note: The following films are secular films that do not contain Christian values but do show realistic stepfamily situations. Some of the language is explicit, and situations may not be morally acceptable to you. Please use your own judgment before watching these films.

Autumn Heart, starring Ally Sheedy and Tyne Daly, Ventura, 2001. This film, while it contains a lot of graphic language, portrays the real heartache experienced by three adult daughters and one grown son of parents who split up and split the children up when they were very young.

When the daughters find their now-grown brother and father after their mom has a heart attack, they discover that the divorce was not as cut-and-dried as they had imagined and that each of their parents had faults. Sheedy gives a particularly gripping performance as a daughter angry at her father's desertion, when she finds out that the truth is not what she has always believed.

The climactic scene with Sheedy's character realizing the truth and facing her father is a strong object lesson for any parent who is tempted to block a former spouse's contact with their children. It shows in painful detail the lasting damage alienation causes.

Stepmom, starring Julia Roberts and Susan Sarandon, Columbia/Tristar, released to video in 1999. This film deals with a terminally ill mom (Sarandon) having to work through her anger and grief toward the new stepmother in her children's lives who will be raising them after her death.

Fiction Books

Covenant Child by Terri Blackstock, W Publishing, 2002.

Blackstock tells the story of twins taken away from a stepmother following their father's death and their long journey home. An excellent portrayal of a stepmother as a loving, warm individual with her family's best interests at heart.

Seasons series by Terri Blackstock and Beverly LaHaye, Zondervan, 1999–2002.

This four-book fiction series begins with Seasons Under Heaven *and includes* Times and Seasons, Showers in Season, *and* Season of Blessing. *It follows four neighboring families in their journeys of faith. One family has a single, divorced mom who finds love again along the way and faces the challenges of a new stepfamily.*

Nonfiction Books

Boundaries by Dr. Henry Cloud and Dr. John Townsend, Zondervan, 1992.

Cloud and Townsend have created an entire series of books, audio products, and seminars on establishing appropriate boundaries around the relationships in your life. These are excellent tools for many areas and include Boundaries with Kids, Boundaries and Teenagers, Boundaries in Marriage, *and more.*

Can Stepfamilies Be Done Right? by Joann Webster and
Seth Webster, Creation House, 2001.

> *This book written by a stepmother and stepson
> covers the bases of stepfamily matters and tells the
> true story of the wayward stepson who found his way
> home.*

Caution: Dangerous Devotions by Jackie Perseghetti,
Chariot Victor, 1995.

> *This devotional series includes quick, witty, humorous
> daily readings perfect for families on the go or with short
> attention spans. These readings teach truth in quick bites
> appropriate for all ages.*

Creative Correction by Lisa Whelchel, Tyndale House,
2000.

> *The former Facts of Life television star is now a
> stay-at-home, homeschooling mom of three who offers
> valuable parenting insight and truly creative ways for
> disciplining children and imparting truths.*

Dad's Everything Book for Daughters by John Trent, Ph.D.,
Zondervan, 2002.

Dad's Everything Book for Sons by John Trent, Ph.D., and
Greg Johnson, Ph.D., Zondervan, 2003.

> *These books are packed with practical advice and
> creative ways dads can connect with their children to
> make them feel special and loved.*

Family Traditions by J. Otis Ledbetter and Tim Smith,
Cook, 1998.

> *This book is part of the "Heritage Builders" series and
> encompasses a variety of ways you can build traditions in
> your family or stepfamily to create a legacy of faith and
> fun.*

Growing Kids God's Way by Gary Ezzo and Anne Marie Ezzo, Growing Families International, 1994.

The Ezzos have an entire parenting curriculum taught at churches around the country. The course also offers workbooks and audiotapes, plus stepfamily and single-parent supplements.

Helping Those Who Hurt by H. Norman Wright, Bethany House, 2003.

This brilliant book gives insight into helping friends in need.

Heritage Builders series by Jim Weidmann and various authors, Chariot Victor, 1998–99.

Heritage Builders are great family devotional workbooks designed to get families up and moving, their brains and hands engaged in each activity and practical lesson. Topics range from holidays to money matters.

Keep the Siblings, Lose the Rivalry by Dr. Todd Cartmell, Zondervan, 2003.

Dr. Cartmell's book offers encouragement for the sibling journey plus practical tips for parents with warring children.

Kids Hope by Gary Sprague, Cook, 1997.

Gary Sprague grew up in a single-parent home and has created a series of workbooks and seminars to help kids express the emotions that come with divorce. His seminars, held in churches throughout the country, are excellent.

Loving a Prodigal: A Survival Guide for Parents of Rebellious Children by H. Norman Wright, Chariot Victor, 1999.

Loving Someone Else's Child by Angela Elwell Hunt, Tyndale House, 1992.

A popular fiction author and adoptive mother, Hunt passes along wisdom regarding embracing and loving other people's children, whether it be one's stepchildren, nieces, grandchildren, or adopted family members.

Manners Matter by Hermine Hartley, Promise Press, 2002.

This little book covers everything from phone manners to sportsmanship. It is a great tool for stepfamilies needing to instill respect.

Mom's Everything Book for Daughters by Becky Freeman, Zondervan, 2002.

Mom's Everything Book for Sons by Becky Freeman, Zondervan, 2003.

This time it is Mom's turn to find creative ways to connect with her daughters and sons.

Passport to Purity by Dennis and Barbara Rainey, FamilyLife, 1999.

This program is a weekend getaway kit for a parent to be able to prepare an adolescent for growing up. Audiotapes provide lessons on sexuality, peer pressure, dating, and other topics, while parents are guided through hands-on illustrations to drive points home. The kit includes a guidebook for adults, audiotapes, a workbook for the adolescent, a passport, and gold seals. This program has been a wonderful addition to our family.

The Power of a Praying . . . series by Stormie Omartian.

Omartian's best-selling series on prayer includes The Power of a Praying Parent, The Power of a Praying Wife, and others.

Relief for Hurting Parents by Buddy Scott, Allon, 1994.

This is the best book I have ever read for parents who

are dealing with out-of-control teenagers. Scott offers words of wisdom that address subjects from choosing a counselor to dealing with juvenile detention centers. Scott is affirming and encouraging. Consider this a must-read.

The Smart Stepfamily: Seven Steps to a Healthy Family by Ron L. Deal, Bethany House, 2002.

Ron L. Deal, stepfamily author, speaker, and founder of Successful Stepfamilies, provides seven effective, achievable steps toward building a healthy marriage and a workable and peaceful stepfamily. Developed from Deal's national seminars on the topic, this book is equally useful for couples, individuals considering remarriage, small groups, and ministry leaders.

Simply Romantic Nights, by Dennis Rainey et al., FamilyLife, 2000.

This boxed kit includes small workbooks and sets of sealed note cards for husbands and wives that contain recipes for a romantic evening. Also includes stickers to put on your calendars as reminders of the specially designed date nights. Lots of sexy fun!

Stepfamilies: Love, Marriage, and Parenting in the First Decade by Dr. James H. Bray and John Kelly, Broadway Books, 1998.

Bray and Kelly's study is the first comprehensive study of stepfamilies over a ten-year period and provides some fascinating and encouraging insights.

Strengthening Your Stepfamily by Elizabeth Einstein and Linda Albert, American Guidance Service, 1986.

This workbook covers all the bases, from preparing for remarriage to creatively handling finances. The book is filled with cute cartoons and easy-to-read charts that make the information readily accessible.

Teknon and the Champion Warriors by Brent Sapp, Family-Life, 2000.

Written as a graphic novel (comic-book format), Teknon and its companion workbook offer fathers and sons a journey through adolescence together with character-building truths along the way.

Traveling Light by Max Lucado, W Publishing, 2001.

Max Lucado's examination of the Twenty-third Psalm is unlike any other. He reminds us to unpack our suitcases of worries, guilt, and regrets, and follow our Shepherd to a place of rest.

"What My Parents Did Right!" compiled by Gloria Gaither, Howard, 2002.

Gloria Gaither has compiled stories from Larnelle Harris, Sandi Patty, Kay Arthur, Frank Peretti, and many more to bring together the "best of the best" in parenting traditions and tips.

The World's Easiest Guide to Finances by Larry Burkett with Randy Southern, Northfield, 2000.

This easy-to-use workbook is packed with steps toward financial freedom by Christian financial expert Larry Burkett. It comes with an interactive budgeting CD-ROM.

The Wounded Spirit by Frank Peretti, W Publishing, 2001.

Frank Peretti tells his emotional autobiography and pleads with popular, beautiful people to protect those who are weaker than they are.

"You Can't Make Me!" (But I Can Be Persuaded) by Cynthia Ulrich Tobias, Waterbrook, 1999.

Tobias specializes in learning styles and personality

differences. Her writing and audiotapes are funny and filled with wisdom.

Magazines

Your Stepfamily: Embrace the Journey
    http://www.yourstepfamily.com
    This magazine is the official magazine of the Step-family Association of America. It is free for members of the SAA.

Seminars and Ministry Resources

Ron L. Deal conducts seminars for stepfamilies at churches throughout the country. For more information, visit www.successful stepfamilies.com.

FamilyLife conducts marriage conferences called Weekend to Remember (a full weekend event) and Rekindling the Romance (a one-day seminar) throughout the country. Visit www.familylife.com for more information.

Focus on the Family holds one-day women's conferences called Renewing the Heart that can reenergize drained moms and stepmoms. Visit www.family.org or www. renewingtheheart.com for more information.

Natalie Nichols Gillespie is a mom and stepmom of seven who speaks on stepfamilies and homeschooling. For more information, contact natalieg@tampabay.rr.com.

Gary Sprague conducts divorce recovery seminars for children throughout the country. Visit www.kidshope. org for more information.

Divorce Care, www.divorcecare.com, offers support

groups all over the country to help hurting adults recover and heal from their divorces.

DC4K (Divorce Care 4 Kids) is an excellent program designed to teach church leaders how to help kids work through their family's divorce. Get more information at www.dc4k.org.

Websites

Blended Families Need StepHeroes
http://www.blended-families.com
Emily Bouchard, MSSW, acts as a personal coach to help stepparents and stepfamilies.

Blending a Family Ministry
www.blendingafamily.com
Moe and Paige Becnel are founders of Blending a Family Ministry. It is their desire to see all blended families find God's plan and God's best for their lives. Their ministry focuses on helping each family to become a true, loving family; to provide a solid foundation for their children; and to establish this through God's love, mercy, and grace.

Changing Families
www.changingfamilies.com
Changing Families offers support for one-parent families, as well as educational classes for parents involved in family litigation.

Creative Connections Ministry
www.creativeconnectionsministry.com

Don and Kathy Coryell operate this faith and grace-based ministry dedicated to both preparing couples for remarriage and strengthening and vitalizing existing marriages and stepfamilies.

Designing Dynamic Stepfamilies
www.designingdynamicstepfamilies.com
Gordon and Carri Taylor of Opportunities Unlimited have a heart for seeing stepfamilies "bring the pieces to peace" through their popular seminars, DVD workshops, and curriculum.

FamilyLife
http://www.familylife.com
The web page for the popular syndicated Christian radio show, marriage conferences, and family-building resources, FamilyLife is backed by popular authors and speakers Dennis and Barbara Rainey. Resources can also be obtained by calling 800-FL-TODAY (800-358-6329).

Fathers.com
http://www.fathers.com
The site for The National Center for Fathering, founded in 1990 by Dr. Ken Canfield. It offers lots of good resources for dads.

Happy Stepfamily Day
http://www.happystepfamilyday.org
This site celebrates Stepfamily Day, September 16, a day when families across the United States hold picnics and celebrate their stepfamily.

Home School Legal Defense Association
http://www.hslda.org

You don't have to be a homeschooler to appreciate this site, which is packed with information on laws that affect families, as well as homeschooling laws and resources.

InStep Ministries
www.instepministries.com

Husband and wife team Jeff and Judi Parziale are dedicated to serving the community by providing practical and biblical resources, support, and counsel to single, divorced, and remarried individuals, their families, and the churches who minister to them. Their vision is to see every single, single-parent, and stepfamily member connected to and serving in a grace-based community of faith.

Marriage Savers
http://www.marriagesavers.org

Mike and Harriet McManus founded Marriage Savers in 1996 as a ministry that equips local communities, principally through local congregations, to help men and women to prepare for lifelong marriage, strengthen existing marriages, and restore troubled marriages.

National Stepfamily Resource Center
www.stepfamilies.info

The National Stepfamily Resource Center's primary objective is to serve as a clearinghouse of information, resources, and support for stepfamily members and the professionals who work with them.

Stepfamily in Formation
http://www.sfhelp.org

This nonprofit educational divorce-prevention site provides more than seven hundred web pages of detailed information. These articles and worksheets stem from twenty-five years of professional research on how to avoid and resolve most divorced-family and stepfamily problems and build better relationships.

Successful Stepfamilies
http://www.successfulstepfamilies.com

Resources for church and home from stepfamily educational and ministry expert Ron L. Deal. At this site churches can order curriculum and stepfamilies can find practical resources including books, videos, and articles to download. In addition, you can link to other sites, register for a Tele-Class, or find a live stepfamily conference near you.

Notes

Introduction

1. U.S. Bureau of the Census (1998), *Marital Status and Living Arrangements, Current Population Reports* (series P20-514), Washington, DC: Government Printing Office.

2. J. Larson, "Understanding Stepfamilies," *American Demographics* 14 (1992): 360.

Chapter 2: Look Both Ways Before Crossing the Threshold

1. Ron L. Deal, *The Smart Stepfamily: Seven Steps to a Healthy Family* (Minneapolis: Bethany House, 2002), 25.

Chapter 3: The Honeymoon Is Over: Renewing the Romance

1. Gary Ezzo and Anne Marie Ezzo, *Growing Kids God's Way* (Chatsworth, CA: Growing Families International, 1994).

2. Tim LaHaye and Beverly LaHaye, *The Act of Marriage* (Grand Rapids: Zondervan, 1976).

3. Dennis Rainey et al., *Simply Romantic Nights* (Little Rock: FamilyLife, 2000).

4. Willard F. Harley, *His Needs, Her Needs: Building an Affair-Proof Marriage* (Grand Rapids: Fleming H. Revell, 1986).

5. For more on love languages, I highly recommend Dr. Gary D. Chapman's *The Five Love Languages* (Chicago: Northfield Publishing, 1992), *The Five*

Love Languages of Teenagers (Chicago: Northfield Publishing, 2000), and *The Five Love Languages of Children* (Chicago: Northfield Publishing, 1997). All can be found online or at your local Christian bookstore.

Chapter 5: Dialing Kids Direct: Getting Emotional Long-Distance

1. Deal, *The Smart Stepfamily*, 26.

Chapter 7: Learning to Love When You Don't Even Like: Falling in Love with All the Children in Your Home

1. Elizabeth Einstein and Linda Albert, *Strengthening Your Stepfamily* (Circle Pines, MN: American Guidance Service, 1986), 54–55.

2. Lynn Vale, "Your Stepladder to Success," *Stepfamilies Quarterly* (Fall 1992) http://www.saafamilies.org/education/articles/sm/vale.htm.

Chapter 8: The Divided Highway of Discipline: Who Does It, When, Where, and How?

1. James H. Bray and John Kelly, *Stepfamilies: Love, Marriage, and Parenting in the First Decade* (New York: Broadway Books, 1998), 42.

2. Ibid., 120.

3. Lisa Whelchel, *Creative Correction* (Wheaton: Tyndale House, 2000).

Chapter 9: New Kids on the Block: Brothers and Sisters, Unite!

1. Frank Peretti, *The Wounded Spirit* (Nashville: W Publishing, 2001).

Bibliography

Bray, James H., and John Kelly. *Stepfamilies: Love, Marriage, and Parenting in the First Decade.* New York: Broadway Books, 1998.

Cartmell, Todd. *Keep the Siblings, Lose the Rivalry.* Grand Rapids: Zondervan, 2003.

Deal, Ron L. *The Smart Stepfamily: Seven Steps to a Healthy Family.* Minneapolis: Bethany House, 2002.

Einstein, Elizabeth, and Linda Albert. *Strengthening Your Stepfamily.* Circle Pines, MN: American Guidance Service, 1986.

Ezzo, Gary, and Anne Marie Ezzo. *Growing Kids God's Way.* Chatsworth, CA: Growing Families International, 1994.

Hunt, Angela Elwell. *Loving Someone Else's Child.* Wheaton: Tyndale House, 1992.

Lofas, Jeanette, with Dawn B. Sova. *Stepparenting: Everything You Need to Know to Make It Work!* New York: Kensington, 1985.

Scott, Buddy. *Relief for Hurting Parents*. Lake Jackson, TX: Allon, 1994.

Visher, Emily. *How to Win as a Stepfamily*. New York: Brunner/Mazel Trade, 1991.

Webster, Joann, and Seth Webster. *Can Stepfamilies Be Done Right?* Lake Mary, FL: Creation House, 2001.

Whelchel, Lisa. *Creative Correction*. Wheaton: Tyndale House, 2000.

Wright, H. Norman. *Helping Those Who Hurt*. Minneapolis: Bethany House, 2003.

Natalie Nichols Gillespie is a wife, mom, stepmom, and adoptive mom of seven who homeschools her younger children and finds time to contribute to Christian magazines such as *Christian Parenting Today*, *HomeLife*, and *Today's Christian*. She also edits for several publishing houses, and enjoys judging the annual Christy Awards and speaking about stepfamilies, adoption, and homeschooling. She lives with her stepfamily in Weeki Wachee, Florida, home of the world-famous mermaids. She welcomes feedback at natalienichols32@yahoo.com.